EMERIL LAGASSE
POWER AIR FRYER 360 COOKBOOK

800 Days of Healthy And Delicious Air Fryer Recipes to AirFry, Bake, Rotisserie, Dehydrate, Toast, Roast, and Slow Cook

Gale Robertson

Copyright © 2021 by Gale Robertson

All Right Reserved.

ISBN: 979-8748297332

Under no circumstances, no part of this publication may be reproduced, distributed, or transmitted in any form or by any means, including photocopying, recording, or other electronic or mechanical methods, or by any information storage and retrieval system without the prior written permission of the copyright holder.

The information in this book is accurate and complete, however, the author and the publisher do not warrant the accuracy of the information, text and graphics contained within the book due to the rapidly changing nature of science, research, known and unknown facts and internet. The author and the publisher do not hold any responsibility for errors, omissions or contrary interpretation of the subject matter herein. This book is presented solely for motivational and informational purposes only.

CONTENTS

INTRODUCTION 8

SNACKS & SIDE DISHES 13

   Salmon Croquettes 13
   Effortless Chicken Croquettes 14
   Crunchy Rutabaga Chips 14
   Eggplant Fries 15
   Tasty Mozzarella Sticks 16
   Quick Parsnip Crisps 16
   Stuffed Mushrooms 17
   Breaded Chicken Tenderloins 18
   Bacon Corn on the Cob 18
   Pecorino Sticks 19
   Baby Carrot Fries 20
   Classic Onion Rings 20
   Egg & Cheese Sandwich 21
   Mediterranean Cheesy Watermelon 22
   Dill Salmon Cakes 22
   Baked Eggplant Chips with Yogurt Sauce 23
   Pancetta & Egg Cups 24
   Avocado Fries with Mustard-Mayo Dip 24
   Italian Sausage Bowl 25
   Turkey & Bacon Pizza Calzone 26
   African-Style Turkey Meatballs 27
   Spicy Roasted Nuts 28
   Mini Bacon Omelet Rolls 28

Sausage Frittata with Cherry Tomatoes 29
Mushrooms & Turkey Sandwich 29
Deli Ham & Cheese Bread Pudding 31
Soy Sauce Omelet 32

VEGETARIAN AND VEGAN 33

Crispy Brussels Sprouts with Hot Aioli 33
Easy Vegetable Bites 34
Traditional Chickpea Falafel 35
Spring Onion & Corn Patties 36
Cheese & Veggie Stuffed Mushrooms 36
Crunchy Cauliflower Florets 37
Savory Mozzarella Wraps 38
Tex-Mex Tacos 38
Cabbage & Tofu Sandwich 39
Bell Pepper Dip Sauce 40
Vegetable Pasta 40
Avocado Egg Wraps 41
Brussels Sprouts with Hazelnuts 42
Favorite Stuffed Peppers 42
Cheese Stuffed Butternut Squash 43
Easy Vegetable Skewers 44
Parsley Mushrooms 45

POULTRY RECIPES 46

Parmesan Chicken Thighs 46
Picante Chicken Parmesan with Tomato Topping 47
Juicy Chicken Breasts 48
Hot Chicken Wings 49

Chili Chicken Skewers 50
Stuffed Chicken with Pancetta & Lemon 51
Classic Buffalo Chicken with Blue Cheese 52
Effortless Chicken Lollipop 53
Herb & Garlic Stuffed Whole Chicken 54
Sunday Stuffed Whole Chicken 55
Corn Flaked Chicken Bites 56
Prosciutto-Wrapped Chicken 56
Curry Chicken Drumsticks 57
Basic Rotisserie-Style Chicken 58
Moroccan-Style Chicken with Yogurt Sauce 59
Mustard Chicken Breasts 60
Paprika Chicken Patties 60
Chicken Goujons 61
Allspice Roasted Chicken 62
Caribbean Sesame Chicken Wings 63
Baked Turkey with Eggs 64

PORK RECIPES 65

Breaded Pork Chops 65
Bacon-Wrapped Pork Tenderloin 66
Pork Burgers 67
Roasted Pork Belly 68
Kabobs with Pork & Veggie 69
Marinated Pork Chops 70
Garlic Pork Rack 71
Sausage Rolls with Bacon 72
BBQ Pork Ribs 73

BEEF & LAMB RECIPES 74

Spiced Beef Roast 74
Beef Breaded Strips 74
Beef Schnitzel 75
Traditional Beef Burgers 76
Beef Steak with Olive Tapenade 77
Teriyaki Beef Steak 78
Herbed Beef Meatballs 78
Cholula Rack Rib Steak 79
Beef Steak with Chimichurri 80
Mustard New York Strip 80
Beef Meatloaf 81
Beef Kebab with Indian Sauce 82
Rib Eye Steak 82
Old-Fashioned Beef Stroganoff 83
Roasted Steak with Herb Butter 84
Beef Enchilada Bake 84
Beef Steak Bites 85
Korean Roast Beef 86
Mushroom & Beef Steak with Egg Noddles 86
Mexican Beef Rolls 87
Roasted Beef with Russet Potatoes 88
Oregano Lamb Chops 89

FISH & SEAFOOD 90

Speedy Dilled Salmon 90
Cod Fillets with Fennel & Pecans 90
Smoked Trout Frittata 91

- Classic Louisiana-Style Crab Cakes 92
- Tuna Cake Burgers 92
- Tasty Salmon with & Cheese 93
- Alaskan Salmon with Green Sauce 94
- Crispy Fish Fingers 94
- Spanish-Style Calamari Rings 95
- Peanut Butter Shrimp 96
- Italian Shrimp Risotto 96
- Parsley Crab Cake Burgers 97
- Authentic Gingery Shrimp 98
- Rich Old Sailors' Drunken Mussels 99

DESSERTS 100

- Roasted Pineapples 100
- Festive Buttermilk Cookies 100
- Lime Cupcakes 101
- Vanilla-Chocolate Biscuits 102
- Cherry Pie 102
- Berry-Yogurt Cups 103
- Honey Bread Pudding 104
- Chocolate & Pineapple Cake 104
- Italian-Style Pancakes 105
- Snickerdoodle Cookies 106
- Fried Banana Dessert 106
- French Toast 107

INTRODUCTION

In today's world, there's a lot of sensitization about eating not just good foods but also healthful ones. This explains why many people are paying particular attention to how their foods are prepared. With this, one ensures they are eating tasty foods while eradicating bad cholesterol as much as possible.

One of the ways to do this is and still enjoy rich flavor is by using the famous air fryer ovens. They are the perfect partner to get tasty and healthy foods. The Emeril Lagasse 360 air fryer oven stands right at the top for convenience, efficiency and versatility, which is great for frying, roasting, and baking.

Emeril Lagasse 360 air fryer oven also provides a better replacement for all your toaster, food dehydrator, convection oven, toaster oven, deep fryer, slow cooker, standalone air fryer, and microwave at the same time. With its 360 quick-cook technology, you are sure to get quick and tasty results from your effortless cooking.

How it works

The Emeril Lagasse 360 air fryer oven has the above-mentioned 360 quick-cook technology and five heating elements that work to circulate hot air through the use of a fan across the food items. This even circulation of hot air ensures that the food is cooked simultaneously from all angles giving it a crispy and crunchy result.

The oven also has many preset cooking functions that help you to automatically set the time and temperature for your cooking. With the preset buttons, you don't have to bother about the right temperature or time - it will cook your meal for you. Nonetheless, you can change these settings yourself depending on your cooking desire, crispness or doneness.

Benefits of using the Emeril Lagasse 360 air fryer oven

1. **It Offers Great Versatility:** There's hardly anything that makes someone as happy as having a multi-functioning kitchen appliance. The ease that comes with using an air fryer to dehydrate, air fry, roast, and toast is just countless. The oven has an LCD Digital Display with 12 Cooking Functions. With these air fryers, you don't have to worry about getting different kitchen appliances for all the types of cooking you will like to try out. You can use it to replace your toaster, food dehydrator, convection oven, toaster oven, deep fryer, slow cooker, standalone air fryer, and microwave. This Emeril Lagasse 360 air fryer is nothing short of a super appliance, combining different cooking styles and giving you the best.

2. **No Worries About Your Health:** There is far less concern about your health using this oven rather than traditional frying pans which are known for their excessive oil or fat usage. This excessive oil and fat are what this appliance helps you eradicate. For instance, this air fryer can help you reduce unhealthy calories in your meals by up to 70% while maintaining great taste. With this air fryer, you have no fear of "hidden" fats and calories. As such, health conditions such as heart diseases, high amounts of cholesterol, and inflammation are drastically reduced.

3. **It Comes With Air Fryer Accessories Sets:** The Emeril Lagasse 360 Air Fryer Oven comes with different accessories set you need for the cooking that you might want to do. It has a 3-pc. crisper tray set, rotisserie spit, rotisserie stand, 2-pc. Pizza rack set, baking pan, and drip tray. It also has a cookbook written by the eminent Chef Emeril. No doubt, this will guide your cooking adventure in extraordinary ways.

4. **Improved Technology:** One prominent thing that separates this air fryer from the conventional oven is that it is made with improved technology and construction design. Hence, it is better than the usual toaster ovens. This air fryer has a 360° Quick Cook Technology and five super-powerful heating elements. This means that it cooks your food evenly with super-heated air, ensuring that crispy texture. What's more? With its high watt-power air fryer, it cooks your meal 40% faster.

5. **Assured Quality:** This multi-purpose Emeril Lagasse 360 air fryer oven is made with top-quality materials to ensure durability. This appliance has a chef-quality design and construction that will make it last longer throughout many seasons. It also has preset cooking functions that allow you to customize your cooking to your desired result.

Best Foods For Frying, Roasting, and Baking

Yes, one of the things that stand the Emeril Lagasse 360 air fryer oven out is its versatility. You can use it to fry, roast, and bake many of your favorite food items. Some of the yummiest foods you can cook are:

Doughnuts, Chicken wings, Roast Beef, Fish, Poultry, Pizza, Pies, Cookies, Cakes, Bread, and other delicious meals (you'll find tons of them in the recipes below).

Common Errors and Mistakes

So far, you have seen how to use the Emeril Lagasse 360 air fryer oven, how it works, and what you stand to gain. What's next? You are eager to start baking, roasting, or air frying with it. Well, that's a great thing to do, but take a step back and consider some common mistakes people make while using the appliance.

This would not only save you from making the same mistakes but also increase your user experience. Here's some of them:

Applying Oil: Usually, people are supposed to know that this is an air fryer and doesn't need oil. But, it seems they are used to the common practice of using oil to roast or fry their foods. The Emeril Lagasse 360 air fryer oven does not need oil during the circulation of hot air. So, if you don't want to miss out on that crispy and crunchy taste you have always longed for, then do away with the oil. Some recipes may call for oil, but usually that it before cooking and happens outside the air fryer oven.

Immediately Placing Food Items Inside: Of course, you might feel the urge to want to quickly use your appliance and get back to other things. But this is not the best practice. Some things need to be done before placing food in it. One of such is preheating the air fryer before putting your food in it. This will not only make your food turn out tasty and crispy, but it will also make the process faster.

Putting A Large Number of Food In The Air Fryer: Everyone and everything has a limit. You do, so also does the Emeril Lagasse 360 air fryer oven. Even though the appliance has a large room for many foods, you should not put too much at a time. Try as much as possible to reduce the number of foods you put at a go. Usually, a turkey weighing as much as 8-10 pounds could be roasted but always check not to overcrowd food.

Tips and Tricks

The Emeril Lagasse 360 comes relatively easy for everyone because it has been made to be as much user-friendly as possible. But then, it's always great to know some tips and tricks that will save you time and efforts. Sounds good?

- Do not clean or store this appliance immediately after use. Instead, allow it to cool down. You don't go to sleep after an exercise; you first shower and cool down. So let your Emeril Lagasse 360 air fryer oven cool down before cleaning it and storing it.

- Ensure you clean the appliance after use. Please pay attention to cleaning the exterior with a wet cloth and the interior with some warm water and sponge in cleaning. Using these will give your appliance a fresh and thorough cleaning.

- Pay attention to the interior components of the air fryer oven like pans, baskets, and some other removable parts. You should wash all these and dry them clean before reusing them.

- Sometimes you will have some food items stick to the pans and make it messy. In such a situation, just soak the pan in some warm water to loosen the stuck food. After this, you can then get down to washing.

- When kitchen appliances are stuffed together, there might be risk of getting overheated and catching fire. Worse still, the fire could spread so fast because of the stuffed appliances. You don't want this for your kitchen. So, as much as possible, ensure you give enough space around your appliance when it's working.

- The connection cord is an important power link for the air fryer. As such, ensure you keep it from wearing out. Check the cable too, and keep it intact.

- There might be some situations of your air fryers emitting smoke during use. This might cause you to want to panic but don't. There's a simple way to bring it under control. What you have to do is to quickly turn it off and allow it to cool. In most situations, the cause of the smoke is always some grease. Trace it and wipe it out.

- You might be tempted to overstuff your air fryers with food items because you are running out of time. Sadly, experience has shown that this will overweight the appliance and might cause it to deteriorate faster. To ensure you enjoy your appliance, avoid doing this. Also, properly stuff your food items in the air fryers before you begin using the appliance.

We finally have an overview of what the Emeril Lagasse Air Fryer Oven is and how it can make your life in the kitchen better, cleaner and tastier. Without further ado, let's get into our delicious recipes, so you can enjoy your air fryer oven as soon as possible!

SNACKS & SIDE DISHES

Salmon Croquettes

Prep + Cook Time: 20 minutes + chilling time | **Servings**: 4

Ingredients

1 (15-oz) tinned salmon, deboned and flaked

1 cup grated onion

1 ½ cups grated carrots

3 large eggs

1 ½ tbsp chopped chives

4 tbsp mayonnaise

4 tbsp breadcrumbs

2 ½ tsp Italian seasoning

Salt and black pepper to taste

2 ½ tsp lemon juice

Directions

In a bowl, add salmon, onion, carrots, eggs, chives, mayo, crumbs, Italian seasoning, pepper, salt, and lemon juice and mix well.

With hands, form 2-inch thick oblong balls from the mixture, resembling croquette shape.

Put them in the refrigerator for 45 minutes.

Preheat your Emeril Lagasse oven to 400 F on Air Fry function.

Grease the frying basket with cooking spray.

Remove the croquettes from the fridge and arrange them in a single layer on a frying basket without overcrowding. Spray with cooking spray.

Cook in your Emeril oven for 10 minutes, flipping once, until crispy.

When cooking is complete, remove the pan from the oven.

Serve with a dill-based dip.

Effortless Chicken Croquettes

Prep + Cook Time: 20 minutes | **Servings**: 4

Ingredients

4 chicken breasts

1 whole egg

Salt and black pepper to taste

1 cup oats, crumbled

½ tsp garlic powder

1 tbsp parsley

1 tbsp thyme

Directions

Pulse chicken breast in a processor food until well blended.

Add seasoning to the chicken alongside garlic, parsley, and thyme and mix well. In a bowl, add beaten egg and beat until the yolk is mixed.

In a separate bowl, add crumbled oats. Form croquettes using the chicken mixture and dip in beaten egg, and finally in oats until coated.

Preheat your Emeril Lagasse oven to 360 F on Air Fry function.

Place the nuggets in the frying basket. Press Start/Pause to begin cooking. Cook for 10 minutes, making sure to keep shaking the basket after every 5 minutes.

When cooking is complete, remove the pan from the oven. Serve and enjoy!

Crunchy Rutabaga Chips

Prep + Cook Time: 20 minutes | **Servings**: 2

Ingredients

1 rutabaga, sliced

1 tsp olive oil

1 tsp soy sauce

Salt to taste

Directions

Preheat your Emeril Lagasse oven to 400 F on Air Fry function.

In a bowl, mix oil, soy sauce, and salt to form a marinade.

Add rutabaga pieces and allow to stand for 5 minutes.

Press Start/Pause to begin cooking. Cook in the oven for 5 minutes, tossing once halfway through cooking.

When cooking is complete, remove the pan from the oven.

Serve with yogurt dip.

Eggplant Fries

Prep + Cook Time: 20 minutes | **Servings**: 3

Ingredients

2 eggplants

¼ cup flour

¼ cup olive oil

½ cup water

Directions

Preheat your Emeril Lagasse oven to 390 F on Air Fry function.

Cut the eggplants in slices of half-inch each.

In a big bowl, mix the flour, olive oil, water, and eggplants; slowly coat the eggplants.

Cook for 12 minutes or until they start to brown. Repeat the process until all eggplant slices are cooked.

When cooking is complete, remove the pan from the oven. Serve with yogurt or tomato sauce. Enjoy!

Tasty Mozzarella Sticks

Prep + Cook Time: 40 minutes | **Servings**: 2

Ingredients

8 oz mozzarella cheese

1 tsp garlic powder

1 egg

1 cup breadcrumbs

½ tsp salt

Olive oil for greasing

Directions

Cut the mozzarella into 6 strips. Whisk the egg along with the salt and garlic powder in a bowl. Dip mozzarella strips into the egg mixture first and then into the breadcrumbs.

Arrange them on a platter and place in the freezer for about 20 to 30 minutes.

Preheat your Emeril Lagasse oven to 370 F on Air Fry function.

Grease the fryer basket with olive oil. Arrange the mozzarella sticks inside. Press Start/Pause to begin cooking.

Cook for 5 minutes. Make sure to turn them over at least 2 times to ensure even cooking until golden on all sides.

Serve with marinara sauce. Enjoy!

Quick Parsnip Crisps

Prep + Cook Time: 15 minutes | **Servings**: 3

Ingredients

6 large parsnips

⅓ cup olive oil

⅓ cup cornstarch

⅓ cup water

1 pinch of salt

Directions

Preheat your Emeril Lagasse oven to 390 F on Air Fry function.

Peel and cut the parsnips to ½ inch by 3 inches.

Mix the cornstarch, olive oil, water, and parsnips in a large bowl. Combine the ingredients and coat the parsnips.

Place in the oven. Press Start/Pause to begin cooking. Fry the parsnips for around 12 minutes.

When cooking is complete, remove the pan from the oven. Serve and enjoy!

Stuffed Mushrooms

Prep + Cook Time: 20 minutes | **Servings**: 2

Ingredients

2 tbsp olive oil

Salt and black pepper to taste

10 button mushrooms

2 cups mozzarella, chopped

2 cups cheddar cheese, chopped

3 tbsp mixture of Italian herbs

1 tbsp dried dill

Directions

Preheat your Emeril Lagasse oven to 340 F on Air Fry function.

In a bowl, mix oil, salt, black pepper, herbs, and dill to form a marinade.

Add button mushrooms to the marinade and toss to coat well.

In a separate bowl, mix both kinds of cheese. Stuff each mushroom with the cheese mixture. Place the mushrooms in the frying basket.

Press Start/Pause to begin cooking. Cook for 10 minutes.

When cooking is complete, remove the pan from the oven. Serve and enjoy!

Breaded Chicken Tenderloins

Prep + Cook Time: 15 minutes | **Servings**: 4

Ingredients

2 tbsp vegetable oil

2 oz breadcrumbs

1 large whisked egg

4 chicken tenderloins

Directions

Preheat your Emeril Lagasse oven to 360 F on Air Fry function.

Combine the vegetable oil with the crumbs.

Keep mixing and stirring until the mixture gets crumbly. Dip the chicken in the egg wash.

Dip the chicken in the crumbs mix, making sure it is evenly and thoroughly covered. Cook for 12 minutes.

When cooking is complete, remove the pan from the oven.

Serve the dish and enjoy its crispy taste with Dijon mustard.

Bacon Corn on the Cob

Prep + Cook Time: 20 minutes | **Servings**: 4

Ingredients

4 ears fresh corn, shucked and cut into halves

2 bacon slices

½ tsp chili powder

Salt and black pepper to taste

½ tsp lemon juice

½ tsp garlic powder

1 tsp olive oil

1 tsp fresh parsley, chopped

1 avocado, peeled and pitted

Directions

Preheat your Emeril Lagasse oven to 400 F on Air Fry function. Press Start/Pause to begin cooking. Cook the bacon in the oven for 6 minutes; chop into small chunks and reserve.

Grease the corn with cooking spray. Place in the fryer. Reduce the temperature to 390 F. Cook the corn for 8 minutes, turning them over halfway through the cooking time.

When cooking is complete, remove the pan from the oven. Meanwhile, in a bowl, mash the avocado with a fork. Add in chili powder, lemon juice, garlic powder, parsley, salt, and black pepper; stir well to combine. Pour the mixture over the corn on the cob and serve warm.

Pecorino Sticks

Prep + Cook Time: 15 minutes | **Servings**: 6

Ingredients

1 cup marinara sauce

12 sticks mozzarella cheese

¼ cup flour

2 cups breadcrumbs

2 whole eggs

¼ cup Pecorino cheese, grated

Directions

Pour breadcrumbs into a bowl. Beat the eggs in a separate bowl. In a third bowl, mix Pecorino cheese and flour. Dip cheese in the flour mixture, then in eggs, and finally in breadcrumbs.

Place the sticks on a cookie sheet and put them in the freezer for 2 hours.

Preheat your Emeril Lagasse oven to 350 F on Air Fry function. Put the sticks in the frying basket. Press Start/Pause to begin cooking.

Cook for 7 minutes, turning them once. Serve with marinara sauce, and enjoy!

Baby Carrot Fries

Prep + Cook Time: 25 minutes | **Servings**: 4

Ingredients

1 ¼ lb. baby carrots

2 tbsp olive oil

1 tsp cumin seeds

½ tsp cumin powder

½ tsp garlic powder

1 handful cilantro, chopped

Salt and black pepper to taste

Directions

Preheat your Emeril Lagasse oven to 370 F on Air Fry function.

Place the baby carrots in a large bowl. Add cumin seeds, cumin, olive oil, salt, garlic powder, and black pepper, and stir to coat them well.

Place the baby carrots in the basket. Press Start/Pause to begin cooking. Cook for 20 minutes.

When cooking is complete, remove the pan from the oven.

Place the carrots on a platter and sprinkle with chopped cilantro. Serve and enjoy!

Classic Onion Rings

Prep + Cook Time: 30 minutes | **Servings**: 4

Ingredients

2 yellow onions, sliced into rings

½ cup flour

¼ cup cornflour

Salt and black pepper to taste

½ tsp dried oregano

2 eggs

½ cup beer

1 tbsp butter, melted

Directions

Sift the flour into a bowl and add the cornflour, oregano, salt, and black pepper and mix well. In a separate bowl, whisk the eggs and stir in the beer.

Pour the mixture into the flour bowl and mix well until the batter has a pancake-like consistency. Place the breadcrumbs on a plate.

Preheat your Emeril Lagasse oven to 400 F on Air Fry function.

Dip the onion rings in the flour/egg mixture; then, roll in the breadcrumbs. Brush with butter and place in the frying basket.

Press Start/Pause to begin cooking. Cook for 4 to 5 minutes, turning them over halfway through the cooking time. When cooking is complete, remove the pan from the oven. Serve and enjoy!

Egg & Cheese Sandwich

Prep + Cook Time: 10 minutes | **Servings**: 2

Ingredients

1 whole egg

½ cup mozzarella cheese

2 English bacon slice, chopped

2 bread slices

1 tbsp butter

½ Italian seasoning

Directions

Preheat your Emeril Lagasse oven to 310 F on Bake function and adjust the cooking time to 30 minutes. Spread butter on one side of the bread slices.

Whisk the egg in a bowl. Add in the cheese and bacon and mix well. Sprinkle with Italian seasoning. Spread the mixture on top of the bread slice.

Place on a baking pan and insert in the oven. Press Start/Pause to begin cooking.

When cooking is complete, remove the pan from the oven. Serve and enjoy!

Mediterranean Cheesy Watermelon

Prep + Cook Time: 15 minutes | **Servings**: 4

Ingredients

8 thick watermelon slices

12 Kalamata olives

8 oz halloumi cheese

2 tbsp chopped parsley

2 tbsp chopped mint

Juice and zest of 1 lemon

Salt and black pepper to taste

Olive oil for brushing

Directions

Preheat your Emeril Lagasse oven to 350 F on Air Fry function.

Season the watermelon with salt and black pepper and gently brush with olive oil. Place in the frying basket and cook for about 4 minutes.

Brush the cheese with olive oil and add it to the fryer; press Start/Pause. Cook for 4 minutes.

When cooking is complete, remove the pan from the oven.

Place watermelon on a platter and serve with olives and sprinkled with herbs and lemon zest and juice. Serve and enjoy!

Dill Salmon Cakes

Prep + Cook Time: 15 minutes | **Servings**: 2

Ingredients

6 oz tinned salmon

1 large egg

4 tbsp chopped celery

4 tbsp spring onion, sliced

1 tbsp dill, fresh and chopped

½ tbsp garlic powder

5 tbsp breadcrumbs

3 tbsp olive oil

Directions

Preheat your Emeril Lagasse oven to 370 F on Air Fry function.

In a bowl, mix the salmon, egg, celery, onion, dill, and garlic powder. Shape the mixture into golf-ball-sized balls. Roll them in the crumbs. Flatten the balls to make the cakes. Then, transfer them to the Air fryer.

Press Start/Pause to begin cooking. Cook for 10 minutes, flipping once.

When cooking is complete, remove the pan from the oven. Serve with tabasco mayo if desired. Enjoy!

Baked Eggplant Chips with Yogurt Sauce

Prep + Cook Time: 20 minutes | **Servings**: 2

Ingredients

2 eggplants

⅓ cup olive oil

1 tbsp parsley, chopped

Salt to taste

1 garlic clove, minced

1 cup yogurt

Directions

Preheat your Emeril Lagasse oven to 370 F on Air Fry function.

Cut the eggplants into slices of ½-inch each. Carefully coat the eggplants with some olive oil and salt. Arrange them on a baking tray in a single layer. Work in batches. Place in the oven. Press Start/Pause to begin cooking.

Cook in the Air fryer for around 15 minutes or until the eggplant starts to brown. Repeat the process until all eggplant slices are fried. Mix the yogurt with the remaining olive oil, garlic, salt, and garlic in a bowl.

When cooking is complete, remove the pan from the oven. Serve with the yogurt sauce.

Pancetta & Egg Cups

Prep + Cook Time: 35 minutes | **Servings**: 2

Ingredients

1 tbsp butter, softened

4 pancetta slices

4 fresh eggs

2 tsp fresh scallions, chopped

Salt and black pepper to taste

Directions

Preheat your Emeril Lagasse oven to 400 F on Bake function.

Grease the ramekins with butter. Line the bottom and the sides of each with 2 pancetta slices; be sure to cover the edges evenly.

Place any excess pancetta in the bottom of the ramekins. Place the ramekins on a baking pan and slide the pan into the oven.

Bake for 10-15 minutes or until the pancetta is crisp and browned.

Carefully crack an egg into the center of each ramekin and sprinkle with salt and black pepper. Return the pan to the oven. Bake for 8-10 minutes until the yolks are set. When cooking is complete, remove the pan from the oven. Sprinkle the cups with scallions and serve.

Avocado Fries with Mustard-Mayo Dip

Prep + Cook Time: 20 minutes | **Servings**: 2

Ingredients

1 cup panko breadcrumbs

Salt and black pepper to taste

2 Haas avocados, cut into wedges

4 tbsp mayonnaise

1 tsp lemon juice

½ tsp mustard

Directions

Preheat your Emeril Lagasse oven to 400 F on Air Fry function.

In a bowl, mix the panko breadcrumbs, salt, and pepper. Dredge the avocado wedges with the panko mixture and arrange them in a single layer on the greased baking sheet. Cook for 10 minutes, flipping halfway through the cooking time.

Mix the mayonnaise, mustard, lemon juice, salt, and pepper in a small bowl. Serve on the side of the avocado fries. Enjoy!

Italian Sausage Bowl

Prep + Cook Time: 20 minutes | **Servings**: 4

Ingredients

1 lb Italian sausages, chopped

4 eggs

1 cup artichoke hearts, chopped

1 sweet onion, diced

2 cups mozzarella cheese, shredded

Salt and black pepper to taste

Fresh cilantro to garnish

Directions

Place a skillet over medium heat and brown the sausage for a few minutes. Drain any excess fat derived from cooking and set aside.

Preheat your Emeril Lagasse oven to 340 F on Air Fry function. Grease the basket with cooking spray and arrange the sausage on it. Top with onion and artichoke hearts; spread the cheese on top.

In a bowl, beat the eggs, and season with salt and black pepper. Pour the mixture into the casserole. Place the casserole dish in the frying basket. Press Start/Pause to begin cooking. Cook for 15 minutes.

When cooking is complete, carefully remove the casserole. Serve sprinkled with fresh cilantro.

Turkey & Bacon Pizza Calzone

Prep + Cook Time: 20 minutes | **Servings**: 4

Ingredients

One package of Pizza dough

4 oz cheddar cheese, grated

1 oz mozzarella cheese, shredded

1 oz bacon, diced

2 cups cooked turkey, shredded

1 egg, beaten

4 tbsp tomato paste

1 tsp basil

1 tsp oregano

Salt and black pepper to taste

Directions

Preheat your Emeril Lagasse oven to 350 F on Bake function and adjust the cooking time to 10 minutes.

Divide the pizza dough into 4 equal pieces, so you have the dough for 4 small pizza crusts.

Combine the tomato paste, basil, and oregano in a bowl.

Brush the mixture onto the crusts; just make sure not to go all the way, avoid brushing near the edges on one half of each crust; place ½ turkey, and season the meat with some salt pepper. Top the meat with some bacon.

Combine the cheddar and mozzarella and divide between the pizzas, making sure that you layer only one half of the dough.

Brush the edges of the crust with the beaten egg.

Fold the crust and seal with a fork.

Transfer to a baking tray and slide in the Air Fryer oven. Press Start/Pause to begin cooking.

When cooking is complete, remove the pan from the oven. Serve.

African-Style Turkey Meatballs

Prep + Cook Time: 22 minutes | **Servings**: 4

Ingredients

Meatballs:

1 ½ tbsp chopped parsley
1 lb. ground lamb
4 oz ground turkey
1 tbsp chopped mint
1 egg white
2 garlic cloves, chopped

2 tsp harissa
1 tsp pepper
1 tsp salt
¼ cup olive oil
1 tsp cumin
1 tsp coriander

Yogurt:

¼ cup chopped mint
¼ cup sour cream
½ cup yogurt

2 tbsp buttermilk
1 garlic clove, minced
¼ tsp salt

Directions

Preheat your Emeril Lagasse oven to 390 F on Air Fry function.

Combine all meatball ingredients in a large bowl.

Wet your hands and make meatballs out of the mixture; cook them for 8 minutes.

Meanwhile, combine all yogurt ingredients in another bowl.

When cooking is complete, remove the pan from the oven.

Serve the meatballs topped with yogurt sauce, and enjoy!

Spicy Roasted Nuts

Prep + Cook Time: 20 minutes | **Servings**: 6

Ingredients

2 tbsp olive oil

1 cup whole cashews

½ cup almonds

½ cup hazelnuts

½ cup peanuts

Salt and black pepper to taste

½ tsp hot paprika

Directions

Preheat your Emeril Lagasse oven to 350 F on Roast function.

Spread the nuts in a single layer on a baking tray and coat them with olive oil, hot paprika, salt, and pepper. Roast for about 8 minutes, shaking the basket once or twice. Serve chilled, and enjoy!

Mini Bacon Omelet Rolls

Prep + Cook Time: 25 minutes | **Servings**: 4

Ingredients

4 crusty rolls

5 eggs, beaten

A pinch of salt

½ tsp dried thyme

3 strips precooked bacon, chopped

2 tbsp heavy cream

4 Gouda cheese thin slices

Directions

Preheat your Emeril Lagasse oven to 330 F on Bake mode. Cut the tops off the rolls and remove the inside with your fingers. Line the rolls with a slice of cheese and press down, so the cheese conforms to the inside of the roll.

In a bowl, mix eggs with heavy cream, bacon, thyme, salt, and black pepper. Stuff the rolls with the egg mixture. Lay the rolls in the frying basket.

Press Start/Pause to begin cooking. Bake for 8 minutes or until the eggs become puffy and the roll shows a golden brown texture.

When cooking is complete, remove the pan from the oven. Serve and enjoy!

Sausage Frittata with Cherry Tomatoes

Prep + Cook Time: 15 minutes | **Servings**: 1

Ingredients

½ sausage, chopped

Salt and black pepper to taste

A bunch of parsley, chopped

3 whole eggs

1 tbsp olive oil

1 slice bread

4 cherry tomatoes, halved

1 slice bread

2 tbsp Parmesan, shredded

Directions

Preheat your Emeril Lagasse oven to 360 F on Air Fry function.

In a bowl, mix tomatoes, sausages, eggs, salt, parsley, Parmesan cheese, olive oil, and black pepper.

Add the frittata mixture to a baking pan and slide in the oven.

Press Start/Pause to begin cooking.

Cook for 20 minutes or until golden brown. Remove and top with Parmesan cheese.

When cooking is complete, remove the pan from the oven. Serve and enjoy!

Mushrooms & Turkey Sandwich

Prep + Cook Time: 15 minutes | **Servings**: 1

Ingredients

⅓ cup shredded leftover turkey

⅓ cup sliced mushrooms

1 tbsp butter, melted

2 tomato slices

½ tsp red pepper flakes

Salt and black pepper to taste

1 hamburger bun

Directions

Melt half of the butter in a skillet over medium heat and add the mushrooms.

Sauté for 4 minutes. Remove to a plate.

Meanwhile, cut the bun in half and spread the remaining butter on the outside of the bun.

Place the turkey on one half of the bun.

Arrange the sautéed mushrooms on top of the turkey.

Cover with tomato slices and sprinkle with salt, pepper, and red pepper flakes. Top with the other bun half.

Preheat your Emeril Lagasse oven to 350 F on Bake function.

Place the sandwich in the oven.

Press Start/Pause to begin cooking.

Cook for 5 minutes.

When cooking is complete, remove the pan from the oven.

Serve and enjoy!

Deli Ham & Cheese Bread Pudding

Prep + Cook Time: 40 minutes | **Servings**: 4

Ingredients

1 cup frozen potato hash browns, thawed

4 French bread slices, cubed

5 fresh eggs

1 cup milk

½ cup diced deli ham

¼ tsp marjoram

½ cup shredded cheddar cheese

Salt and black pepper to taste

Directions

Preheat your Emeril Lagasse oven to 350 F on Bake function and adjust the cooking time to 30 minutes.

Place the bread cubes and potatoes in a lightly greased baking pan and spread evenly.

In a shallow bowl, whisk the eggs with a fork and add in the milk, ham, cheese, marjoram, salt, and black pepper to taste; whisk again until well incorporated.

Pour the mixture over the bread.

Slide the pan in the Air Fryer oven.

Press Start/Pause to begin cooking.

When cooking is complete, remove the pan from the oven.

The pudding is ready when a cake tester inserted in the center comes out clean and dry.

Let it cool to room temperature.

Serve and enjoy!

Soy Sauce Omelet

Prep + Cook Time: 20 minutes | **Servings**: 1

Ingredients

1 small Japanese tofu, cubed

3 whole eggs

Black pepper to taste

1 tsp coriander

1 tsp cumin

2 tbsp soy sauce

2 tbsp green onion, chopped

1 tbsp olive oil

1 whole onion, chopped

Directions

In a bowl, mix eggs, soy sauce, cumin, pepper, olive oil, and salt. Add cubed tofu to baking forms and pour the egg mixture on top.

Preheat your Emeril Lagasse oven to 400 F on Air Fry function.

Place the prepared forms on a baking tray and insert them in the oven. Press Start/Pause to begin cooking. Cook for 10 minutes.

When cooking is complete, remove the pan from the oven. Serve with a sprinkle of coriander and green onion.

VEGETARIAN AND VEGAN

Crispy Brussels Sprouts with Hot Aioli

Prep + Cook Time: 25 minutes | **Servings**: 4

Ingredients

1 lb brussels sprouts, trimmed and excess leaves removed

Salt and black pepper to taste

1 ½ tbsp olive oil

2 tsp lemon juice

1 tsp powdered chili

3 cloves garlic

¾ cup mayonnaise, whole egg

2 cups water

Directions

Place a skillet over medium heat, add in the garlic cloves with the peels, and roast until lightly brown and fragrant, about 3-4 minutes.

Remove the skillet and place a pot with water over the same heat; bring to a boil. Using a knife, cut the brussels sprouts in half, lengthwise. Add to the boiling water to blanch for 3 minutes. Drain through a sieve and set aside.

Remove the garlic from the skillet to a plate; peel, crush and set aside. Add olive oil to the skillet and light the fire to medium heat on the stove-top.

Stir in the brussels sprouts, season with pepper and salt; sauté for 2 minutes and turn off the heat.

Preheat your Emeril Lagasse oven to 350 F on Air Fry function.

Pour the brussels sprouts into the frying basket. Press Start/Pause to begin cooking. Cook for 5 minutes.

Meanwhile, make the garlic aioli. In a bowl, add mayonnaise, crushed garlic, lemon juice, powdered chili, black pepper, and salt; mix well. Remove the brussels sprouts to a bowl and serve with garlic aioli.

Easy Vegetable Bites

Prep + Cook Time: 1 hour 30 minutes | **Servings**: 13 to 16 bites

Ingredients

1 cauliflower, cut into florets

6 medium carrots, diced

1 broccoli, cut into florets

1 onion, diced

½ cup garden peas

2 leeks, sliced thinly

1 small zucchini, chopped

⅓ cup flour

1 tbsp garlic paste

2 tbsp olive oil

1 tbsp curry paste

2 tsp mixed spice

1 tsp coriander

1 tsp cumin powder

1 ½ cups milk

1 tsp ginger paste

Salt and black pepper to taste

Directions

In a pot, steam all vegetables, except the leek and courgette, for 10 minutes; set aside.

Place a wok over medium heat, and add the onion, ginger, garlic, and olive oil. Stir-fry until onions turn transparent. Add the leek, zucchini, and curry. Stir and cook for 5 minutes. Add all spices and milk; stir and simmer for 10 minutes.

Once the sauce has reduced, add the steamed veggies; mix evenly. Transfer to a bowl and refrigerate for 1 hour.

Preheat your Emeril Lagasse oven to 350 F on Air Fry function. Remove the veggie base from the fridge and mold into bite sizes. Arrange the veggie bites in the frying basket. Press Start/Pause to begin cooking. Cook for 10 minutes. Once ready, serve warm with yogurt sauce.

Traditional Chickpea Falafel

Prep + Cook Time: 25 minutes | **Servings**: 6

Ingredients

2 cups cooked chickpeas

½ cup chickpea flour

1 cup fresh parsley, chopped

Juice of 1 lemon

4 garlic cloves, chopped

1 onion, chopped

2 tsp ground cumin

2 tsp ground coriander

1 tsp chili powder

Directions

Preheat your Emeril Lagasse oven to 360 F on Air Fry function.

In a blender, add chickpeas, flour, parsley, lemon juice, garlic, onion, cumin, coriander, chili, turmeric, salt, and pepper, and blend until well-combined but not too battery; there should be some lumps.

Shape the mixture into 15 balls, press them with your hands, and make sure they are still around.

Spray with oil and arrange them in a paper-lined frying basket; work in batches if needed.

Press Start/Pause to begin cooking.

Cook in the Air Fryer oven for 14 minutes, turning once halfway through.

They should be crunchy and golden.

When cooking is complete, remove the pan from the oven.

Serve and enjoy!

Spring Onion & Corn Patties

Prep + Cook Time: 25 minutes | **Servings**: 6

Ingredients

2 cups corn kernels, drained

2 eggs, lightly beaten

⅓ cup chopped spring onions

¼ cup roughly chopped parsley

½ cup all-purpose flour

½ tsp baking powder

Salt and black pepper to taste

Directions

Preheat your Emeril Lagasse oven to 400 F on Air Fry function.

In a bowl, add corn, eggs, parsley, and onion and season with salt and pepper; mix well to combine.

Sift flour and baking powder into the bowl and stir.

Line the frying basket with baking paper and spoon batter dollops, making sure they are separated by at least an inch.

Work in batches if needed. Press Start/Pause to begin cooking.

Cook in the Air Fryer oven for 10 minutes, turning once halfway through.

Cheese & Veggie Stuffed Mushrooms

Prep + Cook Time: 15 minutes | **Servings**: 3

Ingredients

3 portobello mushrooms

1 tomato, diced

1 small red onion, diced

1 green bell pepper, diced

½ cup grated mozzarella cheese

½ tsp garlic powder

Salt and black pepper to taste

Directions

Preheat your Emeril Lagasse oven to 330 F on Air Fry function.

Wash the mushrooms, remove the stems, and pat them dry. Coat with olive oil.

Combine all the remaining ingredients, except for the mozzarella, in a small bowl. Divide the filling between the mushrooms.

Top the mushrooms with mozzarella. Place in the frying basket. Press Start/Pause to begin cooking. Cook for 8 minutes.

When cooking is complete, remove the pan from the oven.

Serve immediately.

Crunchy Cauliflower Florets

Prep + Cook Time: 20 minutes | **Servings**: 4

Ingredients

1 head cauliflower, cut into florets

2 tbsp olive oil

Salt and black pepper to taste

Directions

Preheat your Emeril Lagasse oven to 360 F on Air Fry function.

In a bowl, toss cauliflower, oil, salt, and black pepper, until the florets are well-coated. Arrange the florets in the frying basket.

Press Start/Pause to begin cooking. Cook for 8 minutes; work in batches if needed.

When cooking is complete, remove the pan from the oven.

Serve the crispy cauliflower in lettuce wraps with chicken and cheese.

Savory Mozzarella Wraps

Prep + Cook Time: 25 minutes | **Servings**: 3

Ingredients

½ lb chopped mozzarella cheese

3 packages Pepperidge farm rolls

1 tbsp softened butter

1 tsp mustard seeds

1 tsp poppy seeds

1 small chopped onion

Directions

Preheat your Emeril Lagasse oven to 350 F on Air Fry function.

Mix the butter, mustard, onion, and poppy seeds. Spread the mixture on top of the rolls.

Cover the bottom halves with the chopped mozzarella cheese. Arrange the rolls in the frying basket of the Air Fryer oven.

Press Start/Pause to begin cooking. Cook for 15 minutes. When cooking is complete, remove the pan from the oven. Serve and enjoy!

Tex-Mex Tacos

Prep + Cook Time: 30 minutes | **Servings**: 3

Ingredients

3 soft taco shells

1 cup kidney beans, drained

1 cup black beans, drained

½ cup tomato puree

1 fresh jalapeño pepper, chopped

1 cup fresh cilantro, chopped

1 cup corn kernels

½ tsp ground cumin

½ tsp cayenne pepper

Salt and black pepper to taste

1 cup grated mozzarella cheese

Guacamole to serve

Directions

Preheat your Emeril Lagasse oven to 340 F on Air Fry function.

In a bowl, add beans, beans, tomato puree, chili, cilantro, corn, cumin, cayenne, salt, and pepper; stir well.

Spoon the mixture onto one half of the taco, sprinkle the cheese over the top, and fold over. Spray the frying basket, and lay the tacos inside.

Press Start/Pause to begin cooking. Cook for 14 minutes until the cheese melts.

When cooking is complete, remove the pan from the oven. Serve hot with guacamole.

Cabbage & Tofu Sandwich

Prep + Cook Time: 20 minutes | **Servings**: 1

Ingredients

2 slices of bread

1 1-inch thick tofu slice

¼ cup red cabbage, shredded

2 tsp olive oil, divided

¼ tsp vinegar

Salt and black pepper to taste

Directions

Preheat your Emeril Lagasse oven to 350 F on Air Fry function. Insert the bread slices in the Air Fryer oven and toast for 3 minutes; set aside. Brush the tofu with 1 tsp oil and slide in the oven.

Press Start/Pause to begin cooking. Cook for 5 minutes on each side.

Combine the cabbage, remaining oil, and vinegar, and season with salt and pepper. Place the tofu on top of one bread slice, place the cabbage over, and top with the other bread slice.

When cooking is complete, remove the pan from the oven. Serve and enjoy!

Bell Pepper Dip Sauce

Prep + Cook Time: 25 minutes | **Servings**: 6

Ingredients

¾ lb green bell peppers

¾ lb tomatoes

1 medium onion

1 tbsp lemon juice

1 tbsp olive oil

½ tbsp salt

1 tbsp cilantro powder

Directions

Preheat your Emeril Lagasse oven to 360 F on Air Fry function. Line the peppers, tomatoes, and onion in the frying basket.

Press Start/Pause to begin cooking. Cook for 5 minutes, then flip and cook for 5 more minutes. Remove them and peel the skin.

Place the vegetables in a blender and sprinkle with salt and coriander powder. Blend to smooth and season with salt and olive oil. When cooking is complete, remove the pan from the oven. Serve.

Vegetable Pasta

Prep + Cook Time: 25 minutes | **Servings**: 6

Ingredients

1 lb penne, cooked

1 zucchini, sliced

1 bell pepper, sliced

1 acorn squash, sliced

4 oz mushrooms, sliced

½ cup Kalamata olives, pitted, halved

¼ cup olive oil

1 tsp Italian seasoning

1 cup grape tomatoes, halved

3 tbsp balsamic vinegar

2 tbsp chopped basil

Salt and black pepper to taste

Directions

Preheat your Emeril Lagasse oven to 380 F on Air Fry function.

Combine bell pepper, zucchini, squash, mushrooms, and olive oil in a large bowl.

Season with salt and pepper. Place in the Air Fryer oven.

Press Start/Pause to begin cooking. Cook the veggies for 15 minutes.

In a large bowl, combine penne, roasted vegetables, olives, tomatoes, Italian seasoning, and vinegar. Sprinkle basil and serve.

Avocado Egg Wraps

Prep + Cook Time: 15 minutes | **Servings**: 5

Ingredients

3 ripe avocados, pitted, peeled

10 egg roll wrappers

1 tomato, diced

Salt and black pepper to taste

Directions

Preheat your Emeril Lagasse oven to 340 F on Air Fry function.

Place all filling ingredients in a bowl; mash with a fork until somewhat smooth. There should be chunks left.

Divide the filling between the egg wrappers. Wet your fingers and brush along the edges. Roll and seal the wrappers.

Arrange them on a lined baking sheet, and place in the oven.

Press Start/Pause to begin cooking. Cook in the Air Fryer oven for 5 minutes.

When cooking is complete, remove the pan from the oven.

Serve with sweet chili dipping.

Brussels Sprouts with Hazelnuts

Prep + Cook Time: 35 minutes | **Servings**: 4

Ingredients

1 ½ lb Brussels sprouts, trimmed and halved

2 tbsp extra-virgin olive oil

3 tbsp roasted chopped hazelnuts

Salt and black pepper to taste

2 tbsp balsamic vinegar

Directions

Preheat your Emeril Lagasse oven to 400 F on Air Fry function.

Whisk the olive oil, salt, and pepper in a large bowl and add the Brussels sprouts; toss to coat. Transfer them to the greased frying basket.

Slide in the oven. Press Start/Pause to begin cooking.

Cook for 20 minutes, shaking once until the sprouts are caramelized.

When cooking is complete, remove the pan from the oven. Place the Brussels sprouts on a serving platter and top with hazel and balsamic vinegar. Serve and enjoy!

Favorite Stuffed Peppers

Prep + Cook Time: 25 minutes | **Servings**: 1

Ingredients

¼ cup cooked quinoa

¼ tsp smoked paprika

1 bell pepper

Salt and black pepper to taste

½ tbsp diced onion

1 tsp olive oil

½ diced tomato + 1 tomato slice

¼ tsp dried basil

Directions

Preheat your Emeril Lagasse oven to 350 F on Air Fry function.

Core and clean the bell pepper. Brush with half of the olive oil on the outside. In a bowl, combine all of the other ingredients, except for the tomato slice and the reserved half teaspoon of olive oil.

Stuff the pepper with the filling and top with the tomato slice. Brush the tomato slice with the remaining olive oil and sprinkle with basil.

Place in the Air Fryer oven. Press Start/Pause to begin cooking. Air fry for 10-15 minutes until thoroughly cooked. When cooking is complete, remove the pan from the oven. Serve and enjoy!

Cheese Stuffed Butternut Squash

Prep + Cook Time: 50 minutes | **Servings**: 3

Ingredients

½ butternut squash

6 grape tomatoes, halved

2 poblano peppers, cut into strips

¼ cup grated mozzarella

2 tsp olive oil, divided

Salt and black pepper to taste

Directions

Preheat your Emeril Lagasse oven to 350 F on Air Fry function. Trim the ends and cut the squash lengthwise. You will only need one half for this recipe. Scoop the flash out to make room for the filling. Brush with 1 teaspoon of olive oil.

Place in the Air fryer oven basket and roast for 30 minutes. Combine the remaining olive oil with tomatoes and poblanos; season with salt and pepper.

Place the peppers and tomatoes into the squash. Press Start/Pause to begin cooking. Cook for 15 minutes. If using mozzarella, add it on top of the squash 2 minutes before the end.

Easy Vegetable Skewers

Prep + Cook Time: 20 minutes | **Servings**: 1

Ingredients

1 large sweet potato

1 beetroot

1 red bell pepper

1 tsp chili flakes

¼ tsp black pepper

½ tsp turmeric

¼ tsp garlic powder

¼ tsp paprika

1 tbsp olive oil

Directions

Soak 3 to 4 skewers until ready to use.

Preheat your Emeril Lagasse oven to 350 F on Air Fry function.

Peel the veggies and cut them into bite-sized chunks.

Place the chunks in a bowl, along with the remaining ingredients; mix until thoroughly coated.

Thread the veggies in this order: potato slice, pepper slice, beetroot slice.

Place in the frying basket.

Press Start/Pause to begin cooking. Cook for 15 minutes.

When cooking is complete, remove the pan from the oven. Serve and enjoy!

Parsley Mushrooms

Prep + Cook Time: 15 minutes | **Servings**: 2

Ingredients

2 cups small mushrooms

2 slices white bread

1 garlic clove, crushed

2 tsp olive oil

2 tbsp parsley, finely chopped

Salt and black pepper

Directions

Preheat your Emeril Lagasse oven to 360 F on Air Fry function.

In a food processor, grind the bread into very fine crumbs.

Add garlic, parsley, and pepper; mix and stir in the olive oil.

Cut off the mushroom stalks and fill the caps with the breadcrumbs.

Pat the crumbs inside the caps to ensure there are no loose crumbs.

Place the mushroom caps, one by one, inside the cooking basket and carefully slide them into the frying basket.

Press Start/Pause to begin cooking.

Cook for 10 minutes or until golden and crispy.

When cooking is complete, remove the pan from the oven.

Serve and enjoy!

POULTRY RECIPES

Parmesan Chicken Thighs

Prep + Cook Time: 30 minutes | **Servings**: 4

Ingredients

½ cup shredded Monterrey Jack cheese

½ cup Italian breadcrumbs

4 chicken thighs

2 tbsp grated Parmesan cheese

½ cup marinara sauce

1 tbsp butter, melted

Directions

Preheat your Emeril Lagasse oven to 380 F on Air Fry function.

Spray the frying basket with cooking spray.

In a bowl, mix the crumbs and Parmesan cheese.

Pour the butter into another bowl. Brush the thighs with butter.

Dip each one into the crumbs mixture until well-coated.

Arrange two chicken thighs in the air fryer and lightly spray with cooking oil.

Cook in the Air Fryer oven for 5 minutes.

Flip over, top with a few tbsp of marinara sauce and shredded Monterrey Jack cheese.

Cook for 4 minutes. Repeat with the remaining thighs.

When cooking is complete, remove the pan from the oven.

Serve and enjoy!

Picante Chicken Parmesan with Tomato Topping

Prep + Cook Time: 35 minutes | **Servings**: 2

Ingredients

½ cup flour

¼ tsp cayenne pepper

2 fresh eggs

½ cup Italian breadcrumbs

2 tbsp Parmesan cheese, grated

2 chicken breasts, halved widthwise

1 cup tomato sauce

¾ cup mozzarella, shredded

Salt and black pepper to taste

Directions

Preheat your Emeril Lagasse oven to 400 F on Air Fry function.

Mix the flour with cayenne pepper, salt, and black pepper on a plate.

In a bowl, beat the eggs with a bit of salt. In a separate bowl, combine the Parmesan cheese and breadcrumbs.

Roll the chicken in the flour mixture, then dip in the eggs, and finally coat in the crumbs.

Spray the air fryer basket generously with cooking spray.

Arrange the breasts inside the frying basket and place in the oven.

Press Start/Pause to begin cooking.

Air Fry for 14-16 minutes, turning once halfway through, until golden brown.

When cooking is complete, remove the basket from the oven.

Pour the tomato sauce over the chicken and sprinkle with mozzarella cheese.

Return to the oven and bake for 5 minutes until the cheese is melted. Serve.

Juicy Chicken Breasts

Prep + Cook Time: 35 minutes | **Servings**: 3

Ingredients

2 chicken breasts

Salt and black pepper to taste

1 cup flour

3 eggs, beaten

½ cup apple cider vinegar

½ tbsp ginger paste

½ tbsp garlic paste

1 tbsp sugar

2 red chilies, minced

2 tbsp tomato puree

1 red pepper

1 green pepper

1 tbsp paprika

4 tbsp water

Directions

Preheat your Emeril Lagasse oven to 350 F on Air Fry function. Put the chicken breasts on a clean flat surface. Cut them into cubes.

In a bowl, mix the flour, eggs, salt, and black pepper. Put the chicken in the flour mixture; mix to coat. Place the chicken in the frying basket, spray with cooking spray. Press Start/Pause to begin cooking. Fry for 8 minutes.

Pull out the basket, shake to toss, and spray again with cooking spray. Keep cooking for 7 minutes or until golden and crispy. Remove the chicken to a plate. Put the red, yellow, and green peppers on a chopping board. Using a knife, cut open and deseed them; cut the flesh in long strips.

In a bowl, add the water, vinegar, sugar, ginger and garlic paste, red chili, tomato puree, and smoked paprika; mix with a fork.

Place a skillet over medium heat and spray with cooking spray. Add the chicken and pepper strips. Stir and cook until the peppers are sweaty but still crunchy.

Pour the chili mixture on the chicken, stir, and bring to simmer for 10 minutes; turn off the heat. Dish the chicken chili sauce into a serving bowl and serve.

Hot Chicken Wings

Prep + Cook Time: 1 hour 40 minutes | **Servings**: 4

Ingredients

2 lb chicken wings

1 tbsp olive oil

3 cloves garlic, minced

1 tbsp chili powder

½ tbsp cinnamon powder

½ tsp allspice

1 habanero pepper, seeded

1 tbsp soy sauce

½ tbsp white pepper

¼ cup red wine vinegar

3 tbsp lime juice

2 scallions, chopped

½ tbsp grated ginger

½ tbsp chopped fresh thyme

⅓ tbsp sugar

½ tbsp salt

Directions

In a bowl, add the olive oil, soy sauce, garlic, habanero pepper, allspice, cinnamon powder, cayenne pepper, white pepper, salt, sugar, thyme, ginger, scallions, lime juice, and red wine vinegar; mix well.

Add the chicken wings to the marinade mixture and coat it well with the mixture.

Cover the bowl with cling film and refrigerate the chicken to marinate for 1 hour.

Preheat your Emeril Lagasse oven to 400 F on Air Fry function.

Remove the chicken from the fridge, drain all the liquid, and pat each wing dry using a paper towel.

Place half of the wings in the basket. Press Start/Pause to begin cooking.

Cook for 16 minutes. Shake once.

Remove onto a serving platter and repeat the cooking process for the remaining wings. Serve.

Chili Chicken Skewers

Prep + Cook Time: 35 minutes | **Servings**: 3

Ingredients

3 chicken breasts

Salt to taste

1 tbsp chili powder

¼ cup maple syrup

½ cup soy sauce

2 red peppers

1 green pepper

7 mushrooms

2 tbsp sesame seeds

1 garlic clove

2 tbsp olive oil

Zest and juice from 1 lime

A pinch of salt

¼ cup fresh parsley, chopped

Directions

Put the chicken breasts on a clean flat surface and cut them into 2-inch cubes with a knife. Add them to a bowl, along with the chili powder, salt, maple syrup, soy sauce, sesame seeds, and spray them with cooking spray.

Toss to coat and set aside. Place the peppers on the chopping board. Use a knife to open, deseed and cut into cubes. Likewise, cut the mushrooms in halves.

Start stacking up the ingredients - stick 1 red pepper, then green, a chicken cube, and a mushroom half. Repeat the arrangement until the skewer is full. Repeat the process until all the ingredients are used.

Preheat your Emeril Lagasse oven to 330 F on Air Fry function.

Brush the kabobs with soy sauce mixture and place them into the greased fryer basket.

Press Start/Pause to begin cooking. Cook for 20 minutes, flipping halfway through cooking.

Meanwhile, mix all salsa verde ingredients in your food processor and blend until you obtain a chunky paste. Remove the kabobs when ready and serve with a side of salsa verde.

Stuffed Chicken with Pancetta & Lemon

Prep + Cook Time: 60 minutes | **Servings**: 4

Ingredients

1 small whole chicken

1 lemon

4 slices pancetta, roughly chopped

1 onion, chopped

1 sprig fresh thyme

Olive oil for greasing

Salt and black pepper to taste

Directions

Preheat your Emeril Lagasse oven to 400 F on Air Fry function.

In a bowl, mix pancetta, onion, thyme, salt, and black pepper.

Pat dry the chicken with paper towels.

Insert the pancetta mixture into the chicken's cavity and press tight.

Put in the whole lemon and rub the chicken's top and sides with salt and black pepper.

Spray the frying basket with olive oil and arrange the chicken inside.

Press Start/Pause to begin cooking.

Cook for 30 minutes, turning once halfway through.

When cooking is complete, remove the pan from the oven.

Serve and enjoy!

Classic Buffalo Chicken with Blue Cheese

Prep + Cook Time: 2 hours 25 minutes | **Servings**: 4

Ingredients

1 lb mini drumsticks

3 tbsp butter

3 tbsp paprika

2 tbsp powdered cumin

¼ cup hot sauce

1 tbsp maple syrup

2 tbsp onion powder

2 tbsp garlic powder

½ cup mayonnaise

1 cup crumbled blue cheese

1 cup sour cream

1 ½ tbsp garlic powder

1 ½ tbsp onion powder

Salt and black pepper to taste

1 ½ tbsp cayenne pepper

1 ½ tbsp white wine vinegar

2 tbsp buttermilk

1 ½ tbsp Worcestershire sauce

Directions

Place a pan over medium heat and melt butter. Add the hot sauce, paprika, garlic, onion, maple syrup, and cumin; mix well. Cook the mixture for 5 minutes or until the sauce reduces. Turn off the heat and let cool.

Put the drumsticks in a bowl, pour half of the sauce over, and mix. Save the remaining sauce for serving. Refrigerate for 2 hours.

Meanwhile, in a jug, add the sour cream, blue cheese, mayonnaise, garlic powder, onion powder, buttermilk, cayenne pepper, vinegar, Worcestershire sauce, pepper, and salt. Using a stick blender, blend the ingredients until they are well mixed.

Preheat your Emeril Lagasse oven to 350 F on Air Fry function.

Remove the drumsticks from the fridge and place in the frying basket. Press Start/Pause to begin cooking. Cook for 15 minutes.

Turn the drumsticks every 5 minutes to ensure that they are evenly cooked.

Remove to a serving bowl and pour the remaining sauce over. Serve with the blue cheese sauce and a side of celery sticks.

Effortless Chicken Lollipop

Prep + Cook Time: 50 minutes | **Servings**: 3

Ingredients

1 lb mini chicken drumsticks

½ tbsp soy sauce

1 tbsp lime juice

Salt and black pepper to taste

1 tbsp cornstarch

½ tbsp minced garlic

½ tbsp chili powder

½ tbsp chopped cilantro

½ tbsp garlic- ginger paste

1 tbsp vinegar

1 tbsp chili paste

½ tbsp beaten egg

1 tbsp paprika

1 tbsp flour

2 tbsp maple syrup

Directions

Mix garlic ginger paste, chili powder, maple syrup, paprika powder, chopped coriander, plain vinegar, egg, garlic, and salt, in a bowl. Add the chicken drumsticks and toss to coat. Stir in cornstarch, flour, and lime juice.

Preheat your Emeril Lagasse oven to 350 F on Air Fry function.

Remove each drumstick, shake off the excess marinade, and place in a single layer in the basket. Press Start/Pause to begin cooking. Cook for 5 minutes.

Slide-out the frying basket, spray the chicken with cooking spray and continue to cook for 5 minutes. Remove onto a serving platter and serve with tomato dip and a side of steamed asparagus.

Serve and enjoy!

Herb & Garlic Stuffed Whole Chicken

Prep + Cook Time: 50 minutes | **Servings**: 2

Ingredients

1 small chicken

1 ½ tbsp olive oil

Salt and black pepper to taste

1 cup breadcrumbs

⅓ cup chopped sage

⅓ cup chopped thyme

2 cloves garlic, crushed

1 brown onion, chopped

3 tbsp butter

2 eggs, beaten

Directions

Rinse the chicken gently, pat dry with a paper towel and remove any excess fat with a knife; set aside.

Melt the butter in a pan over medium heat. Sauté garlic and onion until softened.

Add eggs, sage, thyme, pepper, and salt. Mix well.

Cook for 20 seconds and turn the heat off. Stuff the chicken with the mixture into the cavity.

Then, tie the legs of the spatchcock with a butcher's twine and brush with olive oil. Rub the top and sides of the chicken generously with salt and pepper.

Preheat your Emeril Lagasse oven to 390 F on Roast function. Place the spatchcock into the frying basket.

Press Start/Pause to begin cooking. Roast for 25 minutes.

Turn the chicken over and continue cooking for 10-15 minutes more; check throughout the cooking time to ensure it doesn't dry or overcooks.

When cooking is complete, remove onto a chopping board and wrap it with aluminum foil; let rest for 10 minutes. Serve with a side of steamed broccoli.

Sunday Stuffed Whole Chicken

Prep + Cook Time: 100 minutes | **Servings**: 6

Ingredients

1 whole chicken, 3 lb

2 red and peeled onions

2 tbsp olive oil

2 apricots

1 zucchini

1 apple

2 cloves finely chopped garlic

A freshly chopped thyme sprig

5 oz honey

Juice from 1 lemon

2 tbsp olive oil

Salt and black pepper to taste

Directions

For the stuffing, chop all ingredients into tiny pieces.

Transfer to a large bowl and add the olive oil. Season with salt and black pepper.

Fill the cavity of the chicken with the stuffing without packing it tightly.

Preheat your Emeril Lagasse oven to 340 F on Air Fry function.

Place the chicken in the Air Fryer oven.

Press Start/Pause to begin cooking. Cook for 35 minutes.

Warm the honey and the lemon juice in a large pan; season with salt and pepper. Reduce the temperature of the Air Fryer oven to 320 F.

Brush the chicken with some of the honey-lemon marinade and return it to the fryer oven.

Cook for another 70 minutes; brush the chicken every 20-25 minutes with the marinade.

Garnish with parsley and serve.

Corn Flaked Chicken Bites

Prep + Cook Time: 25 minutes | **Servings**: 4

Ingredients

2 chicken breasts, skinless, cut into 2 pieces each

1 egg, beaten

¼ cup buttermilk

1 cup corn flakes, crushed

Salt and black pepper to taste

Directions

In a bowl, whisk egg and buttermilk. Add in chicken pieces and stir to coat. On a plate, spread the cornflakes out and mix with salt and pepper. Coat the chicken pieces in the cornflakes. Spray the air fryer with cooking spray.

Preheat your Emeril Lagasse oven to 360 F on Air Fry function. Arrange the chicken in an even layer in the frying basket. Press Start/Pause to begin cooking.

Cook for 12 minutes, turning once halfway through. When cooking is complete, remove the pan from the oven. Serve.

Prosciutto-Wrapped Chicken

Prep + Cook Time: 25 minutes | **Servings**: 2

Ingredients

2 chicken breasts

1 tbsp olive oil

Salt and black pepper to taste

1 cup semi-dried tomatoes, sliced

½ cup brie cheese, halved

4 slices thin prosciutto

Directions

Preheat your Emeril Lagasse oven to 360 F on Air Fry function. Put the chicken on a chopping board and cut a small incision deep enough to make stuffing on both. Insert one slice of cheese and 4 to 5 tomato slices into each chicken.

Lay the prosciutto on the chopping board. Put the chicken on one side and roll the prosciutto over the chicken, ensuring both ends of the prosciutto meet under the chicken.

Drizzle olive oil and sprinkle with salt and pepper.

Place the chicken in the frying basket. Press Start/Pause to begin cooking. Cook for 10 minutes.

Turn the breasts over and cook for another 5 minutes.

Slice each chicken breast in half and serve with tomato salad.

Curry Chicken Drumsticks

Prep + Cook Time: 25 minutes | **Servings**: 4

Ingredients

4 chicken drumsticks, boneless, skinless

2 tbsp green curry paste

3 tbsp coconut cream

Salt and black pepper

½ jalapeno chili, finely chopped

A handful of parsley, roughly chopped

Directions

Preheat your Emeril Lagasse oven to 400 F on Air Fry function.

In a bowl, add drumsticks, paste, cream, salt, black pepper, and jalapeno; coat the chicken well.

Arrange the drumsticks in the frying basket.

Press Start/Pause to begin cooking. Cook for 6 minutes, flipping once halfway through.

When cooking is complete, remove the pan from the oven. Serve with cilantro.

Basic Rotisserie-Style Chicken

Prep + Cook Time: 80 minutes + marinating time | **Servings**: 4

Ingredients

1 (3 ½-4 lb) whole chicken

2 tbsp salt

2 cups buttermilk

1 tsp lime juice

3 tbsp butter, melted

1 tbsp paprika

Black pepper and sea salt to taste

Directions

Mix the salt, lemon juice, and buttermilk and mix until the salt is dissolved in a large bowl. Submerge the chicken. Cover the bowl and place it in your refrigerator for 2 hours or overnight.

Remove the chicken from the fridge, discard the marinade, and pat it dry with kitchen towels.

Tie the legs with a butcher's twine and brush with butter. Rub the top and sides of the chicken with paprika, sea salt, and black pepper.

Insert the rotisserie rod through the chicken and attach the forks to secure the rod. Select Roast function on your Emeril Lagasse oven and adjust the temperature to 380 F and the time to 50 minutes. Slide the chicken into the oven. Press Start/Pause. Make sure the chicken rotates as it cooks.

Approximately 10-15 minutes before the end of the suggested cooking time, start checking for doneness using a meat thermometer. Chicken should have an internal temperature of 165 F.

When the chicken is cooked through, remove it from the air fryer oven with the removal tool. Put the chicken on a cutting board and carefully remove the chicken from the rod using gloves. Cover with foil and leave to rest 10-15 minutes before carving. Serve warm.

Moroccan-Style Chicken with Yogurt Sauce

Prep + Cook Time: 80 Minutes + marinating time | **Servings**: 4

Ingredients

2 cups sour cream

Salt and black pepper to taste

3 tbsp olive oil

3 cloves garlic, minced

Yogurt Sauce:

2 tbsp olive oil

Salt to taste

¼ tsp red pepper flakes, crushed

2 tsp harissa seasoning

1 tsp dried dill

1 tsp dried tarragon

1 (4-lb) whole chicken

1 cup full-fat yogurt

1 tsp dried dill weed

Directions

Mix all the sauce ingredients and place in the refrigerator until ready to use. Put the chicken in a large bowl and pour the sour cream over. Cover with a lid and place in the fridge for 2-3 hours. Pull the chicken from the refrigerator and let it sit for 30 minutes at room temperature.

Remove the chicken from the marinade. Tie the legs with a butcher's twine. In a small bowl, whisk the olive oil, garlic, paprika, sage, thyme, tarragon, salt, and pepper to taste. Rub the top and sides of the chicken with the mixture.

Insert the rotisserie rod through the chicken and attach the forks to secure the rod. Select Roast function on your Emeril Lagasse oven and adjust the temperature to 380 F and the cooking time to 60 minutes.

Place the chicken in the air fryer oven. Press Start/Pause to begin cooking.

When cooking is complete, remove the pan from the oven. Cover with foil and leave to rest 10-15 minutes before carving. Serve the chicken with yogurt sauce.

Mustard Chicken Breasts

Prep + Cook Time: 30 minutes | **Servings**: 2

Ingredients

2 tbsp Dijon mustard

1 tbsp maple syrup

2 tsp minced fresh rosemary

Salt and black pepper to taste

2 chicken breasts, boneless, skinless

Directions

Preheat your Emeril Lagasse oven to 380 F on Air Fry function.

In a bowl, mix mustard, maple syrup, rosemary, salt, and pepper.

Rub mixture onto chicken. Spray the air fryer basket generously with cooking spray.

Arrange the breasts inside the frying basket. Press Start/Pause to begin cooking.

Cook for 20 minutes, turning once halfway through.

When cooking is complete, remove the pan from the oven. Serve and enjoy!

Paprika Chicken Patties

Prep + Cook Time: 25 minutes | **Servings**: 4

Ingredients

1 lb ground chicken

½ onion, chopped

2 garlic cloves, chopped

1 egg, beaten

½ cup breadcrumbs

½ tbsp ground cumin

½ tbsp paprika

½ tbsp cilantro seeds, crushed

Salt and black pepper to taste

Directions

Preheat your Emeril Lagasse oven to 380 F on Air Fry function.

In a bowl, mix chicken, onion, garlic, egg, breadcrumbs, cumin, paprika, cilantro, salt, and pepper, with hands; shape into 4 patties.

Grease the frying basket with oil, and arrange the patties inside. Do not layer them. Press Start/Pause to begin cooking. Cook in batches if needed. Cook for 10 minutes, turning once.

When cooking is complete, remove the pan from the oven. Serve.

Chicken Goujons

Prep + Cook Time: 15 minutes | **Servings**: 4

Ingredients

2 chicken breasts, skinless, boneless, cut into nuggets

4 tbsp sour cream

½ cup breadcrumbs

½ tbsp garlic powder

½ tsp cayenne pepper

Salt and black pepper to taste

Directions

Preheat your Emeril Lagasse oven to 360 F on Air Fry function.

In a bowl, add sour cream and place the chicken. Stir well.

Mix the breadcrumbs, garlic, cayenne, salt, and black pepper and scatter onto a plate. Roll up the chicken in the breadcrumbs to coat well. Grease the frying basket with oil.

Arrange the nuggets in an even layer. Press Start/Pause to begin cooking. Cook for 10 minutes, turning once halfway through cooking.

When cooking is complete, remove the pan from the oven. Serve.

Allspice Roasted Chicken

Prep + Cook Time: 75 minutes + marinating time | **Servings**: 4

Ingredients

1 (4 lb) whole chicken

4 tbsp olive oil

1 tbsp ground coriander

2 tsp garlic powder

1 tsp onion powder

1 tsp chili pepper

1 tbsp allspice

Directions

Mix the olive oil, coriander, garlic powder, onion powder, chili pepper, and allspice in a large ziplock bag; shake to combine well.

Place the chicken in the bag and massage to coat.

Transfer to the refrigerator and allow marinating for 30 minutes.

Select Air Fry function on Emeril Lagasse oven.

Press Start/Pause to begin cooking.

Remove the chicken from the bag, place it on the rotisserie rod, and insert it in the air fryer oven.

Roast for 40-50 minutes or until the chicken skin is golden and charred, making sure the chicken rotates as it cooks.

Check for doneness with a meat thermometer.

Remove and let the chicken sit for 10 minutes before serving.

Caribbean Sesame Chicken Wings

Prep + Cook Time: 25 minutes | **Servings**: 4

Ingredients

1 lb chicken wings

2 tbsp sesame oil

2 tbsp maple syrup

Salt and black pepper to taste

3 tbsp sesame seeds

Directions

Preheat your Emeril Lagasse oven to 360 F on Air Fry function.

In a bowl, add wings, oil, maple syrup, salt, and pepper and stir to coat well.

In another bowl, add the sesame seeds and roll the wings in the seeds to coat thoroughly.

Arrange the wings in an even layer inside your frying basket.

Press Start/Pause to begin cooking.

Cook for 12 minutes, turning once halfway through.

When cooking is complete, remove the pan from the oven.

Serve and enjoy!

Baked Turkey with Eggs

Prep + Cook Time: 50 minutes | **Servings**: 3

Ingredients

1 lb turkey breasts

Salt and black pepper to taste

¼ cup chicken soup cream

¼ cup mayonnaise

2 tbsp lemon juice

¼ cup slivered almonds, chopped

¼ cup breadcrumbs

2 tbsp chopped green onion

2 tbsp chopped pimentos

2 boiled eggs, chopped

½ cup diced celery

Directions

Preheat your Emeril Lagasse oven to 390 F on Bake function.

Place the turkey breasts on a clean flat surface and season with salt and pepper. Grease with cooking spray and place them in the frying basket; cook for 13 minutes. Remove turkey back onto the chopping board, let cool, and cut into dices.

In a bowl, add the celery, chopped eggs, pimentos, green onions, slivered almonds, lemon juice, mayonnaise, diced turkey, and chicken soup cream and mix well.

Grease a casserole dish with cooking spray, scoop the turkey mixture into the bowl, sprinkle the breadcrumbs on it, and spray with cooking spray. Put the dish in the frying basket press Start/Pause. Bake for 20 minutes.

When cooking is complete, remove the pan from the oven. Serve.

PORK RECIPES

Breaded Pork Chops

Prep + Cook Time: 25 minutes | **Servings**: 3

Ingredients

3 lean pork chops

Salt and black pepper to taste

2 eggs, cracked into a bowl

1 tbsp water

1 cup breadcrumbs

½ tsp garlic powder

3 tsp paprika

1 ½ tsp oregano

½ tsp cayenne pepper

¼ tsp dry mustard

1 lemon, zested

Directions

Put the pork chops on a chopping board and use a knife to trim off any excess fat. Add the water to the eggs and whisk; set aside.

In another bowl, add the breadcrumbs, salt, black pepper, garlic powder, paprika, oregano, cayenne pepper, lemon zest, and dry mustard. Use a fork to mix evenly.

Preheat your Emeril Lagasse oven to 380 F on Air Fry function. Grease the frying basket with cooking spray.

In the egg mixture, dip each pork chop and then in the breadcrumb mixture.

Place the breaded chops in the fryer.

Press Start/Pause. Close the oven and cook for 12 minutes. Flip to the other side and cook for another 5 minutes.

When cooking is complete, place the chops on a chopping board to rest for 3 minutes before slicing and serving. Serve with a side of vegetable fries.

Bacon-Wrapped Pork Tenderloin

Prep + Cook Time: 40 minutes | **Servings**: 4

Ingredients

16 bacon slices

16 oz pork tenderloin

Salt and black pepper to taste

1 cup spinach

3 oz cream cheese

1 small onion, sliced

1 tbsp olive oil

1 clove garlic, minced

½ tsp dried thyme

½ tsp dried rosemary

Directions

Place the tenderloin on a chopping board, cover it with plastic wrap and pound it using a kitchen hammer to a 2-inches flat and square piece. Trim the uneven sides with a knife to have a perfect square. Set aside on a flat plate. On the same chopping board, place and weave the bacon slices into a square of the pork's size.

Place the pork on the bacon weave and set aside. Put a skillet over medium heat on a stovetop, add olive oil, onions, and garlic; sauté until transparent. Add the spinach, ½ tsp rosemary, ½ tsp thyme, a pinch of salt and black pepper. Stir with a spoon and allow the spinach to wilt. Stir in the cream cheese until the mixture is even. Turn off.

Preheat your Emeril Lagasse oven to 360 F on Air Fry function. Spoon and spread the spinach mixture onto the pork loin. Roll up the bacon and pork over the spinach stuffing.

Secure the ends with as many toothpicks as necessary. Season with more salt and black pepper. Place in the frying basket. Press Start/Pause to begin cooking. Cook for 15 minutes. Flip and cook for another 5 minutes.

When cooking is complete, remove to a clean chopping board. Let sit for 4 minutes before slicing. Serve with steamed veggies.

Pork Burgers

Prep + Cook Time: 35 minutes | **Servings**: 2

Ingredients

½ lb ground pork

1 medium onion, chopped

1 tbsp mixed herbs

2 tsp garlic powder

1 tsp dried basil

1 tbsp tomato puree

1 tsp mustard

Salt and black pepper to taste

2 bread buns, halved

Assembling:

1 onion, sliced into 2-inch rings

1 tomato, sliced into 2-inch rings

2 small lettuce leaves, cleaned

4 slices Cheddar cheese

Directions

In a bowl, mix ground pork, chopped onion, mixed herbs, garlic powder, dried basil, tomato puree, mustard, salt, and black pepper.

Form 2 patties out of the mixture and place them on a plate.

Preheat your Emeril Lagasse oven to 370 F on Air Fry function. Place the pork patties in the frying basket, and cook for 15 minutes.

Slide-out the basket and turn the patties with a spatula. Reduce the temperature to 350 F. Press Start/Pause. Cook for 5 minutes.

When cooking is complete, remove them onto a plate and start assembling the burger. Place two halves of the bun on a clean flat surface.

Add the lettuce in both, then a patty each, followed by an onion ring each, a tomato ring each, and then 2 slices of cheddar cheese.

Cover the buns with their other halves. Serve with ketchup and french fries.

Roasted Pork Belly

Prep + Cook Time: 1 hour 30 minutes | **Servings**: 6

Ingredients

1 ½ lb pork belly

1 ½ tsp garlic powder

1 ½ tsp coriander powder

Salt and black pepper to taste

1 ½ dried thyme

1 ½ tsp dried oregano

1 ½ tsp cumin powder

3 cups water

1 lemon, halved

Directions

Preheat your Emeril Lagasse oven to 400 F on Roast function.

Place the pork in the fryer oven.

Press Start/Pause to begin cooking.

Cook for 1 hour.

In a small bowl, add the garlic powder, coriander powder, salt, black pepper, thyme, oregano, and cumin powder.

After the pork is well dried, poke holes all around it using a fork.

Smear the rub thoroughly on all sides with your hands and squeeze the lemon juice all over it. Leave to sit for 5 minutes.

Put the pork in the center of the frying basket and cook for 30 minutes.

Turn the pork with the help of two spatulas, increase the temperature to 350 F and continue cooking for 25 minutes.

When cooking is complete, remove it and place it on a chopping board to sit for 4 minutes before slicing.

Serve the pork slices with a side of sautéed asparagus and hot sauce.

Kabobs with Pork & Veggie

Prep + Cook Time: 1 hour 20 minutes | **Servings**: 4

Ingredients

1 lb pork steak, cut into cubes

¼ cup soy sauce

2 tsp smoked paprika

1 tsp powdered chili

1 tsp garlic salt

1 tsp red chili flakes

1 tbsp white wine vinegar

3 tbsp steak sauce

Skewing:

1 green pepper, cut into cubes

1 red pepper, cut into cubes

1 yellow squash, cubed

1 green squash, cubed

Salt and black pepper to taste

Directions

In a mixing bowl, add the pork cubes, soy sauce, smoked paprika, powdered chili, garlic salt, red chili flakes, white wine vinegar, and steak sauce.

Mix them using a spoon. Refrigerate them for 1 hour.

After one hour, remove the marinated pork from the fridge. Preheat your Emeril Lagasse oven to 370 F on Air Fry function.

On each skewer, stick the pork cubes and vegetables in the order that you prefer. Have fun doing this.

Once the pork cubes and vegetables are finished, arrange the skewers in the frying basket.

Press Start/Pause to begin cooking.

Cook them for 8 minutes. You can do them in batches.

Once ready, remove them onto a platter and serve with salad.

Marinated Pork Chops

Prep + Cook Time: 2 hours 20 minutes | **Servings**: 3

Ingredients

4 stalks lemongrass, trimmed and chopped

3 slices pork chops

2 garlic cloves, minced

1 ½ tbsp sugar

2 shallots, chopped

2 tbsp olive oil

1 ¼ tsp soy sauce

1 ¼ tsp fish sauce

1 ½ tsp black pepper

Directions

In a bowl, add the garlic, sugar, lemongrass, shallots, olive oil, soy sauce, fish sauce, and black pepper; mix well.

Add the pork chops, coat them with the mixture.

Allow to marinate for around 2 hours to get nice and savory.

Preheat your Emeril Lagasse oven to 400 F on Air Fry function.

Working in batches, remove and shake each pork chop from the marinade and place it in the fryer basket.

Press Start/Pause to begin cooking.

Cook it for 7 minutes.

Turn the pork chops with kitchen tongs and cook further for 5 minutes.

When cooking is complete, remove the pan from the oven.

Serve the chops with a side of sautéed asparagus.

Enjoy!

Garlic Pork Rack

Prep + Cook Time: 50minutes | **Servings**: 4

Ingredients

1 lb rack of pork

2 tbsp olive oil

1 clove garlic, minced

Salt and black pepper to taste

1 cup chopped macadamia

1 tbsp breadcrumbs

1 egg, beaten in a bowl

1 tbsp rosemary, chopped

Directions

Add the olive oil and garlic to a bowl.

Mix vigorously with a spoon to make garlic oil.

Place the rack of pork on a chopping board and brush it with the garlic oil using a brush.

Sprinkle with salt and black pepper.

Preheat your Emeril Lagasse oven to 250 F on Roast function.

In a bowl, add breadcrumbs and rosemary. Mix with a spoon and set aside.

Brush the meat with the egg on all sides and sprinkle the nut mixture generously over the pork. Press with hands.

Put the coated pork in the frying basket.

Press Start/Pause to begin cooking. Roast for 30 minutes.

Increase the temperature to 390 F and cook further for 5 minutes.

Once ready, remove the meat onto a chopping board.

Allow a sitting time of 10 minutes before slicing.

Serve with a side of parsnip fries and tomato dip.

Sausage Rolls with Bacon

Prep + Cook Time: 45 minutes + chilling time | **Servings**: 4

Ingredients

Sausage:

8 bacon strips

8 pork sausages

Relish:

8 large tomatoes

1 clove garlic, peeled

1 small onion, peeled

3 tbsp chopped parsley

A pinch of salt

A pinch of pepper

2 tbsp sugar

1 tsp smoked paprika

1 tbsp white wine vinegar

Directions

Start with the relish; add the tomatoes, garlic, and onion in a food processor. Blitz them for 10 seconds until the mixture is pulpy. Pour the pulp into a saucepan, add the vinegar, salt, black pepper, and place it over medium heat.

Bring to simmer for 10 minutes; add the paprika and sugar. Stir with a spoon and simmer for 10 minutes until pulpy and thick. Turn off the heat, transfer the relish to a bowl, and chill for 1 hour.

Meanwhile, wrap each sausage with a bacon strip neatly and stick in a bamboo skewer at the end of the sausage to secure the bacon ends.

Preheat your Emeril Lagasse oven to 370 F on Air Fry function.

Place 3 to 4 wrapped sausages in the fryer basket. Press Start/Pause to begin cooking. Cook for 12 minutes. Ensure that the bacon is golden and crispy before removing them. Repeat the cooking process for the remaining wrapped sausages. Remove the relish from the refrigerator. When cooking is complete, remove the pan from the oven. Serve the sausages and relish with turnip mash.

BBQ Pork Ribs

Prep + Cook Time: 1 hour 30 minutes | **Servings**: 3

Ingredients

1 lb pork ribs

1 tsp soy sauce

Salt and black pepper to taste

1 tsp oregano

2 tbsp maple syrup

3 tbsp barbecue sauce

2 cloves garlic, minced

1 tbsp cayenne pepper

1 tsp sesame oil

Directions

Put the chops on a chopping board and use a knife to cut them into smaller pieces of desired sizes.

Put them in a mixing bowl. Add the soy sauce, salt, black pepper, oregano, one tablespoon of maple syrup, barbecue sauce, garlic, cayenne pepper, and sesame oil.

Mix well and place the pork in the fridge to marinate in the spices for 1 hour.

Preheat your Emeril Lagasse oven to 350 F on Air Fry function.

Place the ribs in the frying basket. Press Start/Pause to begin cooking.

Cook for 15 minutes.

Turn the ribs using tongs, apply the remaining maple syrup with a brush, close the oven, and cook for 10 more minutes.

When cooking is complete, remove the pan from the oven.

Serve immediately.

BEEF & LAMB RECIPES

Spiced Beef Roast

Prep + Cook Time: 50 minutes | **Servings**: 2

Ingredients

2 tsp olive oil

1 lb beef roast

½ tsp dried rosemary

½ tsp dried thyme

½ tsp dried oregano

Salt and black pepper to taste

Directions

Preheat your Emeril Lagasse oven to 400 F on Air Fry function. Drizzle oil over the beef, and sprinkle with salt, black pepper, and herbs. Rub onto the meat with hands. Place in the oven.

Press Start/Pause to begin cooking. Cook for 45 minutes for medium-rare and 50 minutes for well-done. Check halfway through and flip to ensure they cook evenly.

When cooking is complete, remove the pan from the oven. Wrap the beef in foil for 10 minutes after cooking to allow the juices to reabsorb into the meat. Slice the beef and serve with a side of steamed asparagus.

Beef Breaded Strips

Prep + Cook Time: 25 minutes | **Servings**: 2

Ingredients

2 tbsp vegetable oil

2 oz breadcrumbs

1 whole egg, whisked

½ beef steak, cut into strips

½ whole lemon, juiced

Directions

Preheat your Emeril Lagasse oven to 350 F on Air Fry function.

In a bowl, add breadcrumbs and oil and stir well to get a loose mixture. Dip the strips in the egg, then coat with breadcrumbs.

Place the beef into your frying basket.

Press Start/Pause to begin cooking. Cook for 12 minutes.

When cooking is complete, remove the pan from the oven.

Serve with a drizzle of lemon juice.

Beef Schnitzel

Prep + Cook Time: 25 minutes | **Servings**: 1

Ingredients

2 tbsp olive oil

1 thin beef schnitzel

1 egg, beaten

2 oz breadcrumbs

1 tsp paprika

¼ tsp garlic powder

Salt and black pepper to taste

Directions

Preheat your Emeril Lagasse oven to 350 F on Air Fry function.

Combine olive oil, breadcrumbs, paprika, garlic powder, and salt in a bowl. Dip the beef in with the egg first, and then coat it with the breadcrumb mixture thoroughly.

Line a baking dish with parchment paper and place the breaded meat in. Press Start/Pause to begin cooking. Cook for 12 minutes.

When cooking is complete, remove the pan from the oven. Serve.

Traditional Beef Burgers

Prep + Cook Time: 25 minutes | **Servings**: 4

Ingredients

Beef:

1 ½ lb ground beef

Salt and black pepper to taste

¼ tsp liquid smoke

2 tsp onion powder

1 tsp garlic powder

1 ½ tbsp Worcestershire sauce

Burgers:

4 buns

4 trimmed lettuce leaves

4 tbsp mayonnaise

1 large tomato, sliced

4 slices Cheddar cheese

Directions

Preheat your Emeril Lagasse oven to 370 F on Air Fry function.

In a bowl, combine the beef, salt, black pepper, liquid smoke, onion powder, garlic powder, and Worcestershire sauce using your hands.

Form 3 to 4 patties out of the mixture.

Place the patties in the frying basket; leave enough space between them.

Press Start/Pause to begin cooking. Cook for 10 minutes.

Turn the beef with kitchen tongs, reduce the temperature to 350 F, and cook further for 5 minutes. Remove the patties onto a plate.

When cooking is complete, remove the pan from the oven.

Assemble burgers with lettuce, mayonnaise, sliced cheese, and sliced tomato.

Serve and enjoy!

Beef Steak with Olive Tapenade

Prep + Cook Time: 30 minutes | **Servings**: 4

Ingredients

- 1 red onion, chopped
- 1 clove garlic, minced
- 1 green bell pepper, chopped
- 2 tbsp fresh parsley, chopped
- 2 tbsp capers
- 1 cup black olives, pitted and sliced
- 2 tbsp olive oil
- ½ lemon, juiced
- ½ tsp dried oregano
- 1 ½ pounds sirloin steak
- 2 tbsp olive oil
- Salt and white pepper to taste

Directions

Preheat your Emeril Lagasse oven to 395 F on Air Fry function.

Prepare the olive tapenade by mixing the red onion, garlic, bell pepper, parsley, capers, black olives, lemon juice, salt, white pepper, and remaining olive oil in a bowl.

Keep in the refrigerator until ready to serve.

Season the beef with oregano, salt, and white pepper and drizzle with some olive oil on all sides.

Transfer to the frying basket.

Press Start/Pause to begin cooking.

Cook for 6-8 minutes. Turn the steak and cook further for 8 minutes.

When cooking is complete, remove the steak to a chopping board and let it sit for 3 minutes before slicing.

Serve with olive tapenade on the side.

Teriyaki Beef Steak

Prep + Cook Time: 25 minutes | **Servings**: 3

Ingredients

2 tbsp sesame oil

1 pound sirloin steak, cut into strips

1 tbsp soy sauce

2 tbsp fresh chives, chopped

Black pepper to taste

1 onion, sliced

1 red bell pepper, cut into strips

1 green bell pepper, cut into strips

1 yellow bell pepper, cut into strips

1 cup teriyaki sauce

Directions

Preheat your Emeril Lagasse oven to 400 F on Roast function.

In a bowl, mix the sesame oil, soy sauce, and pepper. Add the steak strips, onion, and bell peppers and stir to combine. Transfer to a lightly greased baking pan.

Cook in your Emeril for 8-10 minutes. Pour the teriyaki sauce all over the beef and vegetables and cook for another 5-8 minutes or until the surface is crispy. Serve topped with fresh chives, and enjoy!

Herbed Beef Meatballs

Prep + Cook Time: 25 minutes | **Servings**: 6

Ingredients

1 small onion, chopped

¾ pound grounded beef

1 tbsp fresh parsley, chopped

½ tbsp fresh thyme, chopped

1 whole egg, beaten

3 tbsp breadcrumbs

Salt and black pepper to taste

Tomato sauce for coating

Directions

Preheat your Emeril Lagasse oven to 390 F on Air Fry function.

In a bowl, mix all ingredients except for tomato sauce. Roll the mixture into 10-12 balls.

Place the balls in the frying basket. Press Start/Pause to begin cooking.

Cook for 8 minutes. Add tomato sauce to the balls to coat and cook for 5 minutes at 300 F.

When cooking is complete, remove the pan from the oven. Gently stir and enjoy!

Cholula Rack Rib Steak

Prep + Cook Time: 35 minutes | **Servings**: 2

Ingredients

- 1 rack rib steak
- Salt to season
- 1 tsp white pepper
- 1 tsp garlic powder
- ½ tsp red pepper flakes
- 1 tsp ginger powder
- 1 cup Cholula hot sauce

Directions

Preheat your Emeril Lagasse oven to 360 F on Air Fry function.

Season the ribs with salt, garlic, ginger, white pepper, and red pepper flakes.

Place the ribs in the frying basket.

Press Start/Pause to begin cooking.

Cook for 15 minutes. Turn the ribs and cook further for 15 minutes.

When cooking is complete, remove the ribs to a chopping board and let sit for 3 minutes before slicing. Plate and drizzle Cholula sauce over and serve.

Beef Steak with Chimichurri

Prep + Cook Time: 30 minutes | **Servings**: 4

Ingredients

1 ½ pounds flank steak

2 tbsp butter

Salt and white pepper to taste

¼ cup olive oil

½ tsp dried oregano

2 tbsp red wine vinegar

½ cup cilantro, chopped

½ cup parsley, chopped

2 garlic cloves

½ tsp chili flakes

Directions

Put the olive oil, oregano, vinegar, cilantro, parsley, garlic, chili flakes, and salt in your food processor and blitz until a thick sauce forms. Set aside.

Preheat your Emeril Lagasse oven to 395 F on Air Fry function.

Season the steak with salt and white pepper and brush it with butter.

Place the steak in your Emeril air fryer oven.

Cook for 14-16 minutes, flipping halfway through the cooking time.

Spoon the chimichurri over the cooked beef and serve. Enjoy!

Mustard New York Strip

Prep + Cook Time: 25 minutes + marinating time | **Servings**: 3

Ingredients

1 pound New York strip

Salt and black pepper to taste

2 tbsp olive oil

1 tsp whole-grain mustard

1 tsp garlic, minced

1 tsp lemon zest

Directions

In a bowl, mix the olive oil, mustard, garlic, lemon zest, salt, and pepper. Add the steak and marinate in the refrigerator for 1 hour.

Preheat your Emeril Lagasse oven to 400 F on Air Fry function.

Place the beef in a lightly greased frying basket. Cook the steaks for 7-8 minutes on each side. Serve.

Beef Meatloaf

Prep + Cook Time: 45 minutes | **Servings**: 6

Ingredients

2 tbsp olive oil

2 green onions, chopped

½ cup mushrooms, chopped

2 pounds ground beef

1 tbsp soy sauce

2 eggs, beaten

1 tbsp Worcestershire sauce

1 potato, peeled and grated

¼ cup ketchup

Directions

Preheat your Emeril Lagasse oven to 360 F on Bake function.

Heat the olive oil in a pan over medium heat.

Sauté the green onions and mushrooms for 4 minutes. Remove to a bowl and let it cool slightly.

Add in the rest of the ingredients, except for the ketchup, and mix well with your hands. Press the mixture into a loaf pan and for 20-25 minutes.

Spread the ketchup on top of the meatloaf and cook for 10 more minutes.

Let it stand on a cooling rack for 5-8 minutes before slicing and serving. Enjoy!

Beef Kebab with Indian Sauce

Prep + Cook Time: 30 minutes + marinating time | **Servings**: 4

Ingredients

1 cup teriyaki sauce

1 ½ pounds sirloin steak, cubed

1 onion, quartered

1 green bell pepper, cut into chunks

Indian Sauce:

1 small cucumber, grated and squeezed

Salt to taste

1 cup full-fat yogurt

¼ cup fresh cilantro, chopped

1 tbsp fresh lime juice

Directions

Mix all the sauce ingredients in a bowl and set aside until ready to serve.

Place the steak cubes in a bowl and cover with half of the teriyaki sauce. Toss to coat and place in the fridge for 1 hour.

Preheat your Emeril Lagasse oven to 400 F on Air Fry function.

Remove the steak cubes from the marinade. Thread them and vegetables onto skewers. Arrange them on a lightly greased frying basket.

Cook for 14-16 minutes, turning halfway through the cooking time. Serve with the previously prepared sauce on the side. Enjoy!

Rib Eye Steak

Prep + Cook Time: 20 minutes | **Servings**: 3

Ingredients

1 pound rib eye, sliced

2 tablespoons butter, melted

Salt and black pepper to taste

2 tbsp soy sauce

Directions

Preheat your Emeril Lagasse oven to 400 F on Air Fry function.

Rub the steak with melted butter, soy sauce, salt, and pepper.

Add to a lightly greased baking pan. Cook for 7 minutes per side.

Serve and enjoy!

Old-Fashioned Beef Stroganoff

Prep + Cook Time: 20 minutes | **Servings**: 3

Ingredients

1 pound thin steak

4 tbsp butter, melted

1 whole onion, chopped

1 cup sour cream

8 oz mushrooms, sliced

4 cups beef broth

16 oz egg noodles, cooked

Directions

In a mixing bowl, mix the melted butter, sliced mushrooms, cream, onion, and beef broth.

Pour the mixture over steak and set aside for 10 minutes.

Preheat your Emeril Lagasse oven to 400 F on Air Fry function.

Place the marinated beef in your frying basket.

Press Start/Pause to begin cooking. Cook for 10 minutes.

When cooking is complete, remove the pan from the oven.

Serve with cooked egg noodles and enjoy!

Roasted Steak with Herb Butter

Prep + Cook Time: 30 minutes | **Servings**: 3

Ingredients

1 pound rib-eye steaks

2 tbsp olive oil

Salt and black pepper to taste

1 garlic clove, minced

½ cup butter, at room temperature

1 tsp fresh parsley, chopped

1 tsp fresh dill, chopped

1 tsp lime zest

Directions

Preheat your Emeril Lagasse oven to 395 F on Roast function.

Season the steaks with salt and pepper and drizzle with olive oil.

Place the steak in your Emeril air fryer oven.

Cook for 7 minutes on each side.

Mix the garlic, butter, parsley, dill, lime zest, salt, and pepper in a bowl.

Spread the herb butter on top of the steaks. Serve and enjoy!

Beef Enchilada Bake

Prep + Cook Time: 20 minutes | **Servings**: 3

Ingredients

2 tsp olive oil

1 lb lean ground beef

2 scallions, chopped

1 cup corn

1 tsp taco seasoning

¼ cup tomatoes, chopped

¼ cup black beans

¼ cup enchilada sauce

3 corn tortillas

¼ cup Mexican cheese, grated

Directions

Preheat your Emeril Lagasse oven to 360 F on Bake function.

Heat the olive oil in a saucepan over medium heat. Add the scallions and garlic and cook for 2 minutes or until tender.

Add the ground beef and cook for a further 3 minutes, crumbling with a spatula. Stir in the enchilada sauce, corn, tomatoes, and black beans.

Sprinkle with taco seasoning. Divide the mixture between the tortillas. Roll up and place in a baking dish. Top with the cheese and bake for 10 minutes until golden on top. Serve with guacamole if desired.

Beef Steak Bites

Prep + Cook Time: 25 minutes | **Servings**: 4

Ingredients

- 1 ½ pounds beef steak, cubed
- 1 tsp dried thyme
- 2 tbsp olive oil
- 1 tsp shallot powder
- 1 tsp garlic powder
- 1 tsp steak seasoning
- ½ tsp cayenne pepper
- Salt and black pepper to taste

Directions

Preheat your Emeril Lagasse oven to 400 F on Roast function.

In a bowl, combine the thyme, olive oil, shallot powder, garlic powder, steak seasoning, cayenne pepper, salt, and pepper; mix well. Add the beef and stir to coat.

Throw in a lightly greased baking tray. Rub the mixture onto the steak. Transfer to the air fryer oven and cook for 14-16 minutes, shaking once or twice until thoroughly cooked. Serve and enjoy!

Korean Roast Beef

Prep + Cook Time: 40 minutes | **Servings**: 4

Ingredients

2 tbsp olive oil

Salt and black pepper to taste

1 ½ pounds roast beef

1 tsp kochukaru (chili pepper flakes)

2 cups white rice, hot cooked

Directions

Preheat your Emeril Lagasse oven to 400 F on Roast function.

Mix the olive oil, kochukaru, salt, and pepper in a bowl. Rub the mixture onto the roast beef. Transfer the beef to a lightly greased frying basket. Roast for 10-12 minutes on each side. Serve over a bed of cooked rice. Enjoy!

Mushroom & Beef Steak with Egg Noddles

Prep + Cook Time: 35 minutes | **Servings**: 5

Ingredients

1 can (14.5-oz) cream mushroom soup

1 ½ pounds beef steak

1 package egg noodles, cooked

1 ounce dry onion soup mix

2 cups mushrooms, sliced

1 whole onion, chopped

½ cup beef broth

3 garlic cloves, minced

Directions

Preheat your Emeril Lagasse oven to 360 F on Air Fry function.

Drizzle onion soup mix all over the meat. In a mixing bowl, mix the sauce, garlic cloves, beef broth, chopped onion, sliced mushrooms, and mushroom soup.

Top the meat with the prepared sauce mixture. Place the prepared meat in the frying basket. Press Start/Pause to begin cooking. Cook for 25 minutes.

When cooking is complete, remove the pan from the oven. Serve with cooked egg noodles.

Mexican Beef Rolls

Prep + Cook Time: 25 minutes | **Servings**: 4

Ingredients

2 tbsp olive oil

1 shallot, chopped

1 ¼ pounds ground beef

½ cup refried beans

1 tsp cumin

1 tsp chili powder

4 corn tortillas

2 tomatoes, chopped

½ cup Mexican cheese, shredded

½ lime, juiced

Salt and black pepper to taste

Directions

Preheat your Emeril Lagasse oven to 350 F on Air Fry function.

Heat the olive oil in a pan over medium heat. Sauté the shallot and ground beef for 4 minutes until the beef is no longer pink and the shallot is translucent.

Remove to a bowl and let it cool slightly.

Add in the beans, cumin, chili powder, lime juice, salt, and pepper and stir to combine. Divide the mixture between the tortillas and top with tomatoes and cheese on top. Roll up the tortillas.

Arrange them on a lightly greased frying basket. Cook for 8-10 minutes, turning halfway through the cooking time.

Serve and enjoy!

Roasted Beef with Russet Potatoes

Prep + Cook Time: 25 minutes | **Servings**: 4

Ingredients

2 tbsp olive oil

4 pound top round roast beef

Salt and black pepper to taste

1 tsp dried thyme

½ tsp fresh rosemary, chopped

2 pounds russet potatoes, halved

Olive oil, pepper and salt for garnish

Directions

Preheat your Emeril Lagasse oven to 360 F on Air Fry function.

In a small bowl, mix rosemary, salt, black pepper, and thyme; rub oil onto the beef. Season with the spice mixture.

Place the prepared meat in your frying basket.

Press Start/Pause to begin cooking. Cook for 20 minutes.

Give the meat a turn and add potatoes, black pepper, and oil.

Cook for 20 minutes more.

Take the steak out and set it aside to cool for 10 minutes.

Cook the potatoes for 10 more minutes and the temperature to 310 F.

When cooking is complete, remove the pan from the oven.

Serve hot.

Oregano Lamb Chops

Prep + Cook Time: 30 minutes | **Servings**: 4

Ingredients

4 lamb chops

1 garlic clove, peeled

1 tbsp + 2 tsp olive oil

1 tbsp fresh oregano, chopped

1 tbsp mint leaves, chopped

Salt and black pepper to taste

Directions

Preheat your Emeril Lagasse oven to 390 F on Air Fry function.

Coat the garlic clove with 1 tsp of olive oil and place in the air fryer.

Press Start/Pause to begin cooking. Cook for 10 minutes.

Meanwhile, mix the herbs and seasonings with the remaining olive oil.

Using a towel or a mitten, squeeze the hot roasted garlic clove into the herb mixture and stir to combine.

Coat the lamb chops with the mixture well and place in the fryer oven.

Press Start/Pause to begin cooking. Cook for 8 to 12 minutes.

When cooking is complete, remove the pan from the oven.

Serve hot.

FISH & SEAFOOD

Speedy Dilled Salmon

Prep + Cook Time: 20 minutes | **Servings**: 4

Ingredients

Cooking spray

4 salmon fillets

½ tsp onion powder

½ tsp garlic powder

1 tbsp dill, chopped

Salt and black pepper to taste

1 lemon, cut into wedges

Directions

Rinse and pat dry the fillets with a paper towel. Coat the fish on both sides with cooking spray. Season with garlic powder, onion powder, salt, and black pepper.

Preheat your Emeril Lagasse oven to 350 F on Air Fry function.

Arrange the fillets skin-side-down in the air fryer oven. Press Start/Pause to begin cooking. Cook for 10 minutes, turning once halfway through cooking.

When cooking is complete, remove the pan from the oven. Sprinkle with dill and serve with lemon wedges.

Cod Fillets with Fennel & Pecans

Prep + Cook Time: 15 minutes | **Servings**: 4

Ingredients

2 black cod fillets

Salt and black pepper to taste

1 cup grapes, halved

1 small fennel bulb, sliced

½ cup pecans

2 tsp white balsamic vinegar

2 tbsp extra virgin olive oil

Directions

Preheat your Emeril Lagasse oven to 400 F on Air Fry function.

Season the fillets with salt and pepper; drizzle oil on top. Place the fillet in the frying basket. Press Start/Pause to begin cooking. Cook for 10 minutes; set the fish aside to cool.

In a bowl, add grapes, pecans, and fennels. Drizzle oil over the grape mixture, and season with salt and pepper. Add the mixture to the basket and cook for 3 minutes. Add balsamic vinegar and oil to the mixture, season with salt and pepper. Pour over the fish and serve.

Smoked Trout Frittata

Prep + Cook Time: 12 minutes | **Servings**: 6

Ingredients

2 tbsp olive oil

1 onion, sliced

1 egg, beaten

6 tbsp crème fraiche

½ tbsp horseradish sauce

2 trout fillet, hot and smoked

A handful of fresh dill

Directions

Heat oil in a frying pan over medium heat. Add onion and stir-fry until tender; season the onions well.

Preheat your Emeril Lagasse oven to 320 F on Air Fry function.

In a bowl, mix egg, crème Fraiche, and horseradish. Add cooked onion and trout, and mix well. Place the mixture in the frying basket. Press Start/Pause to begin cooking. Cook for 20 minutes.

When cooking is complete, remove the pan from the oven. Serve and enjoy!

Classic Louisiana-Style Crab Cakes

Prep + Cook Time: 20 minutes | **Servings**: 4

Ingredients

½ pound jumbo crab

Lemon juice to taste

2 tbsp parsley, chopped

Old bay seasoning as needed

1 tbsp basil, chopped

3 tbsp real mayo

¼ tsp Dijon mustard

Zest of ½ lemon

¼ cup panko breadcrumbs

Directions

Preheat your Emeril Lagasse oven to 400 F on Air Fry function.

In a bowl, mix mayo, lemon zest, old bay seasoning, mustard, and oil. Blend crab meat in a food processor and season with salt. Transfer to the mixing bowl and combine well.

Form cakes using the mixture and dredge the mixture into breadcrumbs. Place the cakes in the frying basket. Press Start/Pause to begin cooking. Cook for 15 minutes.

When cooking is complete, remove the pan from the oven. Serve garnished with parsley and lemon juice.

Tuna Cake Burgers

Prep + Cook Time: 50 minutes | **Servings**: 2

Ingredients

5 oz of canned tuna

1 tsp lime juice

1 tsp paprika

¼ cup flour

½ cup milk

1 small onion, diced

2 eggs

½ tsp salt

1 tsp chili powder, optional

Directions

Place all ingredients in a bowl and mix well to combine. Make two large patties, or a few smaller ones, out of the mixture. Place them on a lined sheet and refrigerate for 30 minutes.

Preheat your Emeril Lagasse oven to 350 F on Air Fry function. Place the patties in the Air Fryer oven. Press Start/Pause to begin cooking. Cook for 7 minutes on each side. When cooking is complete, remove the pan from the oven. Serve and enjoy!

Tasty Salmon with & Cheese

Prep + Cook Time: 15 minutes | **Servings**: 1

Ingredients

1 salmon fillet

1 tsp mustard

3 tbsp pistachios

Sea salt and black pepper to taste

A pinch of garlic powder

1 tsp lemon juice

1 tsp grated Parmesan cheese

1 tsp olive oil

Directions

Preheat your Emeril Lagasse oven to 350 F on Air Fry function. Whisk mustard and lemon juice together. Season the salmon with salt, pepper, and garlic powder. Brush the olive oil on all sides.

Brush the mustard mixture onto salmon. Chop the pistachios finely and combine them with the Parmesan cheese; sprinkle on top of the salmon. Place the salmon in the frying basket with the skin side down. Press Start/Pause to begin cooking. Cook for 12 minutes. When cooking is complete, remove the pan from the oven. Serve and enjoy!

Alaskan Salmon with Green Sauce

Prep + Cook Time: 30 minutes | **Servings**: 4

Ingredients

For Salmon

4 Alaskan wild salmon fillets	A pinch of salt
2 tsp olive oil	

For Dill Sauce

½ cup heavy cream	A pinch of salt
½ cup milk	2 tbsp chopped parsley

Directions

Preheat your Emeril Lagasse oven to 310 F on Air Fry function.

In a mixing bowl, add salmon and drizzle 1 tsp of oil. Season with salt and pepper. Place the salmon in the frying basket.

Press Start/Pause to begin cooking. Cook for 20-25 minutes, until tender and crispy. In a bowl, mix milk, chopped parsley, salt, and whipped cream.

When cooking is complete, remove the pan from the oven. Serve salmon with the sauce. Enjoy!

Crispy Fish Fingers

Prep + Cook Time: 20 minutes | **Servings**: 4

Ingredients

28 oz fish fillets	1 tsp drilled dill
Lemon juice to taste	4 tbsp mayonnaise
Salt and black pepper to taste	1 whole egg, beaten

1 tbsp garlic powder

1 tbsp paprika

3 ½ oz breadcrumbs

Directions

Preheat your Emeril Lagasse oven to 400 F on Air Fry function. Season fish fillets with salt and pepper.

In a bowl, mix beaten egg, lemon juice, and mayonnaise. In a separate bowl, mix breadcrumbs, paprika, dill, and garlic powder. Dredge fillets in egg mixture and then the garlic-paprika mix; repeat until all fillets are prepared.

Place the fillets in the frying basket. Press Start/Pause to begin cooking. Cook for 15 minutes. When cooking is complete, remove the pan from the oven. Serve.

Spanish-Style Calamari Rings

Prep + Cook Time: 20 minutes | **Servings**: 5

Ingredients

12 oz frozen squid

1 tsp cayenne pepper

1 large egg, beaten

Salt and black pepper to taste

1 cup all-purpose flour

Lemon wedges, to garnish

1 tsp ground coriander seeds

Olive oil to spray

Directions

In a bowl, mix flour, ground pepper, paprika, cayenne pepper, and salt. Dredge calamari in eggs, followed by the floured mixture.

Preheat your Emeril Lagasse oven to 390 F on Air Fry function. Place calamari in the oven. Press Start/Pause to begin cooking.

Cook them for 15 minutes until golden brown. Do it in batches if needed to avoid overcrowding. Garnish with lemon wedges, and enjoy!

Peanut Butter Shrimp

Prep + Cook Time: 15 minutes | **Servings**: 5

Ingredients

1 ½ pound shrimp

Juice of 1 lemon

1 tsp sugar

3 tbsp peanut oil

2 tbsp cornstarch

2 scallions, chopped

¼ tsp Chinese powder

1 chili pepper, finely chopped

Salt and black pepper to taste

4 garlic cloves

Directions

Preheat your Emeril Lagasse oven to 370 F on Air Fry function. In a Ziploc bag, mix lemon juice, sugar, pepper, oil, cornstarch, powder, Chinese powder, and salt.

Add in the shrimp and massage to coat evenly. Let sit for 10 minutes. Add garlic cloves, scallions, and chili to a pan and fry for a few minutes over medium heat.

Place the marinated shrimp, garlic, chili pepper, and scallions in the frying basket. Press Start/Pause to begin cooking. Cook for 10 minutes, until nice and crispy.

When cooking is complete, remove the pan from the oven. Serve and enjoy!

Italian Shrimp Risotto

Prep + Cook Time: 25 minutes | **Servings**: 4

Ingredients

4 whole eggs, beaten

Pinch of salt

½ cup rice, cooked

½ cup baby spinach

½ cup Monterey Jack cheese, grated

½ cup shrimp, chopped and cooked

Directions

Preheat your Emeril Lagasse oven to 380 F on Air Fry function.

In a small bowl, add eggs and season with salt and basil; stir until frothy. Spray baking pan with cooking spray. Add rice, spinach, and shrimp to the pan.

Pour egg mixture over and garnish with cheese. Place the pan in the frying basket. Press Start/Pause to begin cooking. Cook for 14-18 minutes until the frittata is puffed and golden brown.

When cooking is complete, remove the pan from the oven. Serve immediately.

Parsley Crab Cake Burgers

Prep + Cook Time: 55 minutes | **Servings**: 4

Ingredients

½ cup cooked crab meat

¼ cup chopped red onion

1 tbsp chopped basil

¼ cup chopped celery

¼ cup chopped red pepper

3 tbsp mayonnaise

Zest of half a lemon

¼ cup breadcrumbs

2 tbsp chopped parsley

Directions

Preheat your Emeril Lagasse oven to 390 F on Air Fry function.

Place all ingredients in a large bowl, and mix well. Make 4 large crab cakes from the mixture and place them on a lined sheet. Refrigerate for 30 minutes to set.

Spray the frying basket with cooking spray and arrange the crab cakes inside.

Press Start/Pause to begin cooking. Cook for 7 minutes on each side until crispy.

When cooking is complete, remove the pan from the oven. Serve and enjoy!

Authentic Gingery Shrimp

Prep + Cook Time: 20 minutes | **Servings**: 4

Ingredients

1 pound shrimp

2 whole onions, chopped

3 tbsp butter

1 ½ tbsp sugar

2 tbsp soy sauce

2 cloves garlic, chopped

2 tsp lime juice

1 tsp ginger, chopped

Directions

In a bowl, mix lime juice, soy sauce, ginger, garlic, sugar, and butter.

Add the mixture to a frying pan and warm over medium heat.

Add in the chopped onions, and cook for 1 minute until translucent.

Pour the mixture over shrimp, toss well, and set aside for 30 minutes.

Preheat your Emeril Lagasse oven to 340 F on Air Fry function.

Place the mixture in the frying basket.

Press Start/Pause to begin cooking.

Cook for 8 minutes.

When cooking is complete, remove the pan from the oven.

Serve and enjoy!

Rich Old Sailors' Drunken Mussels

Prep + Cook Time: 25 minutes | **Servings**: 4

Ingredients

4 pounds mussels

2 tbsp olive oil

1 cup white wine

2 tsp salt

2 bay leaves

1 tbsp pepper

1 ½ cup flour

1 tbsp fenugreek

2 tbsp vinegar

5 garlic cloves

4 bread slices

½ cup mixed

Directions

Preheat your Emeril Lagasse oven to 350 F on Air Fry function.

Add the oil, garlic, vinegar, salt, fenugreek, pepper, and bread to a food processor and process until you obtain a creamy texture.

Add bay leaves, wine, and mussels to a pan.

Bring to a boil over medium heat, lower heat to low, and simmer the mixture until the mussels have opened up.

Take the mussels out and drain; remove from shells.

Add flour to the creamy mixture prepared before.

Cover the mussels with the sauce, slide in the oven.

Press Start/Pause to begin cooking.

Cook them for 10 minutes.

When cooking is complete, remove the pan from the oven.

Serve with fenugreek.

DESSERTS

Roasted Pineapples

Prep + Cook Time: 15 minutes | **Servings**: 2

Ingredients

1 tsp cinnamon

5 pineapple slices

½ cup brown sugar

1 tbsp basil, chopped for garnish

1 tbsp honey

Directions

In a small bowl, mix brown sugar and cinnamon. Drizzle the sugar mixture over your pineapple slices and set aside for 20 minutes.

Preheat your Emeril Lagasse oven to 340 F on Roast function. Place the pineapple rings on a cooking tray. Press Start/Pause to begin cooking.

Roast for 10 minutes. Flip the pineapples and cook for 10 minutes more.

When cooking is complete, remove the pan from the oven. Serve with basil and a drizzle of honey.

Festive Buttermilk Cookies

Prep + Cook Time: 25 minutes | **Servings**: 4

Ingredients

1 ¼ cups flour + some for dusting

½ tsp baking soda

½ cup cake flour

¾ tsp salt

½ tsp baking powder

4 tbsp butter, chopped

1 tsp sugar

¾ cup buttermilk

Directions

Preheat your Emeril Lagasse oven to 400 F on Air Fry function.

Combine all dry ingredients in a bowl. Place the chopped butter in the bowl, and rub it into the flour mixture until crumbed. Stir in the buttermilk.

Flour a flat and dry surface and roll out until half-inch thick. Cut out 10 rounds with a small cookie cutter.

Arrange the biscuits on a lined baking sheet. Press Start/Pause to begin cooking. Cook for 8 minutes.

When cooking is complete, remove the pan from the oven. Let cool completely. Serve and enjoy!

Lime Cupcakes

Prep + Cook Time: 30 minutes | **Servings**: 6

Ingredients

2 eggs plus 1 yolk

Juice and zest of 2 limes

1 cup yogurt

¼ cup superfine sugar

8 oz cream cheese

1 tsp vanilla extract

Directions

Preheat your Emeril Lagasse oven to 330 F on Air Fry function.

Using a spatula, gently combine the yogurt and cheese.

In another bowl, beat together the rest of the ingredients. Gently fold the lime with the cheese mixture. Divide the batter between 6 lined muffin tins.

Press Start/Pause to begin cooking. Cook in the Air fryer oven for 10 minutes.

When cooking is complete, remove the pan from the oven. Serve and enjoy!

Vanilla-Chocolate Biscuits

Prep + Cook Time: 15 minutes | **Servings**: 5

Ingredients

¾ cup flour

¼ tsp baking soda

¾ tsp salt

⅓ cup brown sugar

¼ cup unsalted butter, softened

2 tbsp white sugar

1 egg yolk

½ tbsp vanilla extract

½ cup chocolate chips

Directions

Preheat your Emeril Lagasse oven to 350 F. Line the basket or rack with foil. Whisk flour, baking soda, and salt together in a small bowl. Combine brown sugar, butter, and white sugar in a separate bowl.

Add egg yolk and vanilla extract and whisk until well-combined. Stir flour mixture into butter mixture until dough is just combined; gently fold in chocolate chips.

Scoop dough by the spoonfuls and roll into balls; place onto the foil-lined frying basket, 2 inches apart. Press Start/Pause to begin cooking.

Cook dough in the air fryer until cookies start getting crispy, 5 to 6 minutes. Transfer foil and cookies to wire racks or a plate, and let cool completely. Repeat with the remaining dough. Serve.

Cherry Pie

Prep + Cook Time: 30 minutes | **Servings**: 6

Ingredients

2 store-bought pie crusts

21 oz cherry pie filling

1 egg yolk

1 tbsp milk

Directions

Preheat your Emeril Lagasse oven to 310 F on Air Fry function.

Place one pie crust in a pie pan; poke holes into the crust. Cook for 5 minutes. Spread the pie filling over. Cut the other pie crust into strips and arrange the pie-style over the baked crust.

Whisk milk and egg yolk, and brush the mixture over the pie. Return the pie to the fryer. Press Start/Pause to begin cooking. Cook for 15 minutes.

When cooking is complete, remove the pan from the oven. Serve and enjoy!

Berry-Yogurt Cups

Prep + Cook Time: 30 minutes | **Servings**: 6

Ingredients

1 ½ cups flour

½ tsp salt

½ cup sugar

¼ cup vegetable oil

2 tsp vanilla extract

1 cup blueberries

1 egg

2 tsp baking powder

Yogurt, as needed

Directions

Preheat your Emeril Lagasse oven to 350 F on Air Fry function.

Combine flour, salt, and baking powder in a bowl. In another bowl, add the oil, vanilla extract, and egg. Fill the rest of the bowl with yogurt, and whisk the mixture until fully incorporated. Combine the wet and dry ingredients; gently fold in the blueberries.

Divide the mixture between 10 muffin cups. You may need to work in batches. Cook for 10 minutes. When cooking is complete, remove the pan from the oven. Serve and enjoy!

Honey Bread Pudding

Prep + Cook Time: 45 minutes | **Servings**: 3

Ingredients

8 slices of bread

½ cup buttermilk

¼ cup honey

1 cup milk

2 eggs

½ tsp vanilla extract

2 tbsp butter, softened

¼ cup sugar

4 tbsp raisins

2 tbsp chopped hazel

Cinnamon for garnish

Directions

Beat the eggs along with the buttermilk, honey, milk, vanilla, sugar, and butter. Stir in raisins and hazel. Cut the bread into cubes and place them in a bowl.

Pour the milk mixture over the bread. Let soak for 10 minutes. Transfer to a baking pan.

Preheat your Emeril Lagasse oven to 310 F on Air Fry function and adjust the cooking time to 30 minutes. Place the pan in the Air Fryer oven. Press Start/ Pause to begin cooking.

When cooking is complete, remove the pan from the oven. Garnish with cinnamon to serve.

Chocolate & Pineapple Cake

Prep + Cook Time: 50 minutes | **Servings**: 4

Ingredients

2 oz dark chocolate, grated

8 oz self-rising flour

4 oz butter

7 oz pineapple chunks

½ cup pineapple juice

1 egg

2 tbsp milk

½ cup sugar

Directions

Preheat your Emeril Lagasse oven to 390 F on Air Fry function.

Place the butter and flour into a bowl, and rub the mixture with your fingers until crumbed.

Stir in pineapple, sugar, chocolate, and juice.

Beat eggs and milk separately, and then add to the batter.

Transfer the batter to a previously prepared (greased or lined) cake pan.

Press Start/Pause to begin cooking. Cook for 40 minutes.

Let cool for at least 10 minutes before serving. Enjoy!

Italian-Style Pancakes

Prep + Cook Time: 20 minutes | **Servings**: 4

Ingredients

¼ tsp salt

1 cup all-purpose flour

1 cup milk

1 tsp sugar

3 eggs, beaten

2 tbsp Nutella chocolate

2 tbsp walnuts, chopped

1 tsp lemon zest

Directions

Preheat your Emeril Lagasse oven to 350 F on Air Fry function.

Mix the salt, flour, milk, sugar, eggs, and lemon zest in a bowl. Spoon into a baking pan. Cook for 12-14 minutes, flipping once. Serve topped with Nutella and walnuts

Snickerdoodle Cookies

Prep + Cook Time: 30 minutes | **Servings**: 6

Ingredients

1 can of Pillsbury Grands Flaky Layers Biscuits

1 box instant vanilla Jell-O

1 ½ cups cinnamon sugar

2 tbsp melted butter

Directions

Preheat your Emeril Lagasse oven to 350 F on Air Fry function. Unroll the flaky biscuits; cut them into fourths. Roll each ¼ into a ball. Arrange the balls on a lined baking sheet. Press Start/Pause to begin cooking. Cook in the air fryer oven for 7 minutes or until golden.

Meanwhile, prepare the Jell-O following the package's instructions. Using an injector, inject some of the vanilla pudding into each ball. Brush the balls with melted butter and then coat them with cinnamon sugar. Serve.

Fried Banana Dessert

Prep + Cook Time: 6 minutes | **Servings**: 6

Ingredients

6 bananas

4 large eggs, beaten

1 cup breadcrumbs

1 cup bread flour

1 cup vegetable oil

Directions

Preheat your Emeril Lagasse oven to 350 F on Air Fry function.

Peel the bananas and cut them into pieces of less than 1-inch each.

In a bowl, mix the beaten eggs, bread flour, and vegetable oil. Dredge the banana first into the flour, then dip in the beaten eggs, and finally in the crumbs.

Line the banana pieces in the Air Fryer oven and cook them for 10 minutes, shaking once halfway through.

When cooking is complete, remove the pan from the oven. Serve with vanilla ice cream.

French Toast

Prep + Cook Time: 15 minutes | **Servings**: 4

Ingredients

- 2 eggs, beaten
- 4 slices bread
- 3 tbsp sugar
- 1 ½ cups corn flakes
- ⅓ cup milk
- ¼ tsp nutmeg
- 4 tbsp berry-flavored cheese
- ¼ tsp salt

Directions

In a bowl, mix sugar, eggs, nutmeg, salt, and milk.

In a separate bowl, mix blueberries and cheese. Take 2 bread slices and pour the blueberry mixture over the slices.

Top with the milk mixture. Cover with the remaining two slices to make sandwiches. Dredge the sandwiches over cornflakes to coat well. Lay the sandwiches on a baking tray.

Preheat your Emeril Lagasse oven to 400 F on Bake function.

Place the tray in the oven. Press Start/Pause to begin cooking. Cook for 8 minutes.

When cooking is complete, remove the pan from the oven. Serve with berries and syrup.

Made in the USA
Monee, IL
13 June 2021